A Dinosaur's Guide to Libertarianism

Why Can't They Leave Us Alone?

by
Godfrey Bloom

Grosvenor House
Publishing Limited

All rights reserved
Copyright © Godfrey Bloom, 2019

The right of Godfrey Bloom to be identified as the author of this work has been asserted in accordance with Section 78 of the Copyright, Designs and Patents Act 1988

The book cover is copyright to Godfrey Bloom

This book is published by
Grosvenor House Publishing Ltd
Link House
140 The Broadway, Tolworth, Surrey, KT6 7HT.
www.grosvenorhousepublishing.co.uk

This book is sold subject to the conditions that it shall not, by way of trade or otherwise, be lent, resold, hired out or otherwise circulated without the author's or publisher's prior consent in any form of binding or cover other than that in which it is published and without a similar condition including this condition being imposed on the subsequent purchaser.

A CIP record for this book
is available from the British Library

ISBN 978-1-78623-464-3

Include www.godfreybloom.uk
Facebook: @godfreybloomofficial
Twitter: @goddersbloom

Contents

Acknowledgements	v
Introduction	vii
Chapter 1 - Politicians without Conviction	1
Chapter 2 - Politics, Journalists and Pavlov's Dog	14
Chapter 3 - Why We Cannot Trust Government Statistics	36
Chapter 4 - Everything the State does is inept or incompetent	42
Chapter 5 - Driving	61
Chapter 6 - Law	68
Chapter 7 - The 39 Articles	77
Chapter 8 - The Manipulation of Money	85
Appendix A - How we are governed	93
Appendix B - The Death of Democracy	99
Appendix C - The Socratic Approach	102
Epilogue	111
Bibliography	118

Acknowledgements

It is difficult to know where to start. I paid tribute to many by name in my book 'Billy Nomates'. They have all helped me compile this book, albeit in a less direct way. I must name a few here because without much of their research compiled over many years I would have been struggling. The bibliography is quite extensive for this work and it needed to be. I thank the authors, most alive still, for pioneering in many fields where the establishment fears to tread.

Personal acquaintances and friends include Professor Patrick Barron, Professor Ian Plimer, to the late Mr Keith Peat and Mr Ben Pile. Mises Institute membership has been a godsend, the home now of original in-depth economic comment. I thank all my friends there in Alabama for their guidance and hospitably when I am in the deep south. Thanks also to my old regimental padre Eric Richards (Father Elwin) and some invaluable comment by Wendy Heydorn, a Cambridge University WRFC friend of long standing.

Thanks to the Fórum da Liberdade in Brazil where libertarianism is a blossoming flower and an example to Western Europe so bereft lately of original economic insight. It seems the old world must look now to the new for intellectual example.

I hasten to add that the opinions here are all my own save where acknowledgment is given on the page.

Introduction

Almost no one belongs to a political party. Probably fewer than 0.05% of the electorate. Turn out at European and local elections vary but sometimes only average 30%. Perhaps half the people vote at a general election depending on a range of circumstances and by-elections are a sort of comedy turn in marginal seats and non-events in 'safe' seats. In short, nobody is interested in politics until election time and not even then. If the ballot paper had 'none of the above' on it the support would be overwhelming. Huge numbers of people have told me over the years they 'don't do politics'.

What has astonished me in the last 10 years is how few people even begin to understand how they are governed. Fascinatingly guests around the dinner party table who do express a political opinion are usually those who understand least. I have stopped many a woolly minded 'liberal' or tribal Tory in their tracks by asking them to explain, for those who are not familiar with the system how our laws are made. Just a brief explanation for the assembled guests. Instantly change of subject! Politicians of course rely on this and they are aided and abetted by public service broadcasting and the press. You cannot manipulate or steal from people if they know the tricks. The object of this book is to explain to the layman why their standard of living has stagnated, why their children and grandchildren cannot now expect to enjoy automatically a better life.

As a relative newcomer to politics with a long background in financial services, some modest military experience and fairly broad experience of sport, both playing and sponsoring, in my 70th year, I feel my experience of life is not inconsiderable. I have seen a bit of ducking and weaving especially in the City but nothing plumbs the depths of moral degradation quite like politics and politicians. I do not mean those who have been caught with their hand in the cookie jar. Every profession has its share of people who get confused about what belongs to them and what does not. What is truly awesome is the complete moral and intellectual bankruptcy of far too many of the politicians that I have met. Consider, if you will, the High Court Judgment that a political party manifesto cannot be held in law to be in any way binding on a subsequently elected administration. Imagine any other profession being given dispensation from society's code of conduct or indeed contract law. You go to a restaurant, look at the menu and order your dinner. You expect what is on the menu to arrive, no more, no less. You browse the automobile brochure and order your motor, vorsprung durch technik with a two-litre diesel engine and Harman Kardon wrap around sound in metallic blue. That is what you expect to arrive. You do not pay your cheque and have something completely different delivered to your door because the dealer has now got your money and does not give a shit. You have no legal redress because the dealer's manifesto was only a rough indication of what you might get.

Politicians, European and Westminster have bars with cheaper booze, smoking if you wish, pensions the private sector could only dream of, tax concessions, and travel arrangements at which ordinary folk can only wonder. It is not just elected politicians who make up the political class. They can be sacked by the electorate and vilified without mercy by the press, although the vilification normally comes at the behest of other politicians. There is the significantly more appalling neo-political class. The quango-crats and fake charity bosses. I have been mercilessly lobbied by Christian Aid on corporate tax. Obviously they are pushing a political agenda most big charities now do. It is an intricate game of government self-lobbying. (I was tempted to write self-abuse).

This goes on all the time; it means more infringement of personal liberty, more State theft with the veneer of popular support.

These characters are paid double that which the average politician receives. Same fringe benefits with no electoral accountability.

Try this just for interest. Every time you hear a spokesman come on the early morning news telling us we are too fat, too lazy, drink too much or shouldn't smack our children when they are naughty or complain the middle classes get too much of the educational pie, check out their organisation and find out what they are all earning. They are the great and the good. They exist with political patronage. These appointments are distributed in much the same way as a medieval monarch gave away other people's estates for services rendered.

Regulatory bodies are prime examples. Incidentally the genre fascinate in their ability to almost always be wrong. This is no barrier to even higher officer. The public's protection from all this in days of yore was informed, energetic and investigative press. Oh dear, where did it all go so wrong?

The aim of this book is not an aide memoire on how the British are governed, although my very able ex-colleague, Michael McManus, has produced one in Appendix A. Most readers of this work will already have a broad grasp of that. This is more the work of 'agent provocateur'. It is about why we are governed or certainly why we are governed in the hopelessly inefficient, corrupt and incompetent way we seem to be.

It contains more questions than answers yet I make no apology for that. I believe in the English-speaking world in the last hundred years we have stopped asking appropriate questions, without which we can never find answers, right or wrong.

I am not an academic although I have had plenty of experience lecturing in the academic world. A psychometric assessment years ago for a senior institutional management post marked me as 'clever and articulate but not an intellectual'. I am happy with that, if it be true. I come to the concept of libertarianism therefore with no 'baggage' but I hope now a significant experience of life.

I flick through the potted autobiographies of the leading politicians in the English-speaking world and to me they seem to have no serious achievements or experience outside the narrow field of party politics. Indeed, for all bragging of schools and universities many men and women of my age would not regard them as having had an education in the traditional sense. This becomes obvious whenever they submit to an in-depth interview with someone who has. This is extremely rare for our press and media interviewers, the so-called guardians of our democracy are of the same kidney.

Who has not shouted at the radio and television 'for god's sake why don't you ask him...?' Senior politicians, members of the Royal Family who indulge in politics, churchmen, scientists and educators permanently avoid serious cross-examination because the establishment close ranks. Hectoring, bullying, downright rudeness pass for debate. There are plenty of examples in the following chapters but the reader will already have examples of his own.

One of the inspirers of this book was an airport car park attendant at Leeds who recognised me and stopped for a chat. His main point was simple, 'Why don't they leave us alone?' An ordinary working man had put his finger on the crux of libertarianism and I thank him. Indeed, it could have been the title for this book.

I chose 'A Dinosaur's Guide to Libertarianism' because it has been a favourite word in my consistent and systematic vilification. Classical liberalism and libertarianism is the only possible salvation for mankind; it looks to the future, not the past. For those interested, I suggest they re-visit Hayek's brilliant 1960 lecture entitled 'Why I am not a Conservative'. Or perhaps settle down on holiday with Herbert Spencer's 'Conditions Essential to Human Happiness'.

Chapter 1

Politicians without Conviction

It is not necessary to be an anthropologist to accept that the animal kingdom has a tendency to form groups. Humans are no exception. I took some stick from some of the undergraduates at the Mises Institute after a lecture a few years ago for not supporting the Rothbardian Anarcho view that no formal state is necessary, a view I deeply respect. But 10 years of politics has persuaded me to the concept of the 'art of the possible'. I will return later to the argument because it is legitimate and worthy of discussion.

Gorillas, lions, chimpanzees, wildebeest, dogs, horses, humans all group together in some way. So do, of course, many species of birds and fish. The point at which I drive is that mutual cooperation is a natural state for mankind. I hasten to add that the Anarcho hypothesis does not suggest otherwise.

This grouping manifests itself in many ways. The family is arguably the strongest and has stood the test of time, although in western societies this is under threat; more of that argument later. Our ancestors' families and tribes roamed the planet many thousands of years ago, gradually developing both skills and interactivity. Hunter gatherers worked as teams to their mutual benefit, genetic pre-programming prevented interbreeding, man developed as the dominant species and remains so to the present day. All of this we know, it is unchallenged. Skills, science and trade evolved painfully slowly, civilizations came and went. Empires waxed and waned, indeed usually because they became decadent, non-dynamic or simply overtaken by groups significantly more advanced in science.

Artillery beat spears; indeed the Americas were thus transformed in a remarkably short historical period but superior armament is not enough. Indeed, armaments are societies' tactics, new civilizations evolve often through ideas and innovation. Communism did not fail through a lack of weaponry, indeed quite the reverse. Fascism and National Socialism were at the cutting edge of weapons development. This historical lesson has not yet been learned by the super powers of the Twenty First Century. Aircraft carriers, fighter squadrons, standing armies, missiles and submarines are awesomely expensive yet serve little effective purpose against a terrorist armed with a bomb in his rucksack.

We look back to our primeval ancestors who pooled resources for protection. Arguably in the modern state the prime responsibility is defence of the realm.

Many would suggest that it is the only legitimate role of the state and would encompass defence of trade and in recent times a capacity for retaliation against weapons of mass destruction (don't turn up with a knife to a gun fight). There is no rational argument for any more than enough. The arms race of the twentieth century, particularly the latter part post World War II was absurd and bizarre. Indeed, it took a General to point it out, more of him later too.

Mankind suffers from a dichotomy, as old as time itself. His desire to come together in the spirit of cooperation is as strong as his inclination to exploit a situation in his capacity as an individual. In short, when it comes to crunch time the priority will be self/family first, then tribe, then the common good on any extended concept. Yes, I accept that various religions often influence this assessment but as Damon Runyon said, 'The race is not always to the swift, nor the battle to the strong, but that's the way to bet.'

We understand that the enormous advance in human civilization is based upon division of labour, so well-documented by the work of Adam Smith. We live in a world of the most extraordinary specialisation; trades or professions of yesteryear have been divided, sub-divided again with more to come. Automation that spawned the Luddites of the nineteenth century marches ever onward. Robotics in the future will change even further the society in which we live. It would be a mistake to assume this will only affect the unskilled or semi-skilled. The provincial family lawyer is fast becoming a thing of the past. The law is ever more complex and specialisation therefore more common place. Even the surgeon is not exempt. The orthopaedic specialist of only a few years ago now only 'does' knees, or hip or shoulders or remedial surgery. The motor mechanic of today plugs your car into a machine, no grease monkey he. To the demise of the extended family in the more mobile Anglosphere, the astonishing advances in home entertainment, the disappearance of public houses, community or church-based human association and social clubs have driven people into a sort of bubble. Families no longer even watch TV together. Children view programmes on their own in separate rooms at different times of the day. The traditional Sunday lunch is a thing of the past for most families, let alone the evening meal in decline for some years now. People therefore become self-centred, if not self-obsessed. This in itself has produced a new political dynamic. Economic honesty, reform or an appeal pro bono publico would be electoral suicide. Most folk lurch into the ballot booth to vote the ticket that will do them the least harm, that is if they bother to vote at all. Why would they when all the political parties offer the same bill of fare? Far too many politicians come from the same genre; they too dwell in a bubble, although their bubble is heavily steamed up on the inside, a permanent feature manufactured by their own hot air, hubris, eye to the main chance and craving for office for its own sake.

Democratic Systems

A democratic system monopolised by party political representation is doomed to failure on any number of counts. It is by its very nature exposed to intellectual corruption. A compromise of ideals is the very nature of the beast. Indeed, there are those who regard this as a strength. It is perceived as a foil to extremism. Yet the flaw is in the constitution of the state and what the state's role in society should be. Classic examples of state 'mission creep' abound in the Anglosphere. This begs, as it always must, the question, is limited government actually possible? Hans Hoppe outlines a devastating case that it is simply that those in power will always seek to expand their power base. Lord Acton's well-known view needs no repetition here. Yet the English Bill of Rights and in its offspring, the American constitution, were drafted my men of exceptional foresight. The concept of no taxation without representation is as honoured in principal as it is flouted in practice.

In the United Kingdom, business rates, or property tax if one prefers, is levied on those who are disenfranchised. Enough of these points are made in my essay on electoral reform in the annex. The successful sole proprietor shopkeeper with a pleasant and spacious house can easily find himself liable for £10,000 per year in rates. He is entitled to one vote. A student or welfare dependent is equally entitled to one vote.

The political party has to pander to the 75% to get elected under this system. Curtailment of public spending therefore, or indeed any serious reform cannot be brought about by democratic means. Bankruptcy or revolution are the only options.

My own party embarked on a classical liberal, libertarian ticket. The more success the party enjoys, the more the principles are abandoned. The iniquitous, immoral and foolhardy addiction of the British main parties to progressive taxation is a case in point. For the first time at a UKIP economic committee meeting I heard the phrase 'we cannot sell it on the doorstep'. This, mark you, from a party that has shot to prominence by dealing only with truth in the European Union, single currency and immigration. It is the truth on the doorstep that will and eventually must win. Post war welfarism, both corporate and social, has been so long part of the political landscape, together with a dumbing down of the educational system means this is indeed a difficult sale. Had reform been easy mainstream political parties would have attempted it.

Politicians without conviction, whose only goal is office in the near term at the expense of future generations are of no value.

Eventual breakdown, if history is anything to go by, results not in libertarianism but despotism in some format. Society must therefore be offered an understandable, coherent alternative to the status quo. Yet politicians simply reflect their electorate, if indeed they participate in what is currently simply a charade. Crony capitalism, state broadcasting and vested interest still monopolise the main avenues of communication. With massive public spending the electorate just become clients of the state, unlikely to vote, at odds with what they perceive to be their immediate self-interest.

Ironically these same people of middle England or middle America would be horrified to even consider stealing money from their children's piggy bank to pay for a holiday. No one has yet pointed out to them this is exactly what they are doing.

Libertarianism and Political Parties

When I visit economic or libertarian conferences the debate will always eventually get around to active politics and political parties. There is a strong argument that the true libertarian pure blood should eschew politics and particularly party politics. This is an extremely difficult argument to refute, even if indeed I wished to. Having been a party politician I can only give a view from a personal perspective and leave the reader to make up their own mind.

I spent my professional life as an investment strategist in some form. 1967-2005; it was an enormously varied career, unlikely to be replicated in the future as the grip of specialisation tightens. I have managed funds, sold funds and structured funds for tax advantage and along the way managed people. I have probably been a closet libertarian since I was five. Try a career in the British Army as a libertarian, although the British Army gives more elbow room to the free spirit, maverick or eccentric than I suspect any other army in the world. I remained completely aloof from politics until the mid-nineteen nineties although my father and grandfather were big wigs in local government in the Conservative interest. It is awkward to post-rationalise this because I cannot remember how I felt about party politics throughout my professional career. Of course, I knew the 1970s were a shambles and the 1980s were more successful, but after 1990 there was, nor is there now, any great difference in party policy between the two main UK antagonists Conservative and Labour. At the risk of annoying my many American friends I would argue that the Republican and Democrat policies differ not much. I have not seen a serious brake on government spending in either country for a generation. Administrations are, in the end, a question of taxation, spending and borrowing (yes ok now printing). I think UK government spending reduced in 1987, but otherwise spending has increased exponentially in all other post-war years.

We therefore hear the cry at election time 'vote for the blues, we will waste slightly less of your money than the reds'. An election cry I have mutated for myself in recent elections, with some success, 'Vote for me, I am slightly less of a scoundrel than the others'.

I became a founder member of the United Kingdom Independence Party in the early 1990s. I remain one at the time of writing, albeit somewhat reluctantly. The main policy platform was to lead Great Britain out of the illegal, undemocratic, corrupt, socialist European Union Empire. Paradoxically, although I have been labelled a dinosaur by the British media, as a libertarian there is standing room only when I speak at universities. This is enormously heartening. It means there is a significant body of next generation political activists who are libertarian or at least classical liberal.

There is a powerful school of thought, especially in North America that argues any political involvement is doomed and we must win the battle of the ideas. I understand this point of view and will probably go to my grave still wondering if it is right. What I can argue is that politics for me did two things. It focussed my mind on both libertarianism and classical liberalism. Speaking engagements in some of the world's leading academic institutions and writing articles for leading magazines makes serious study imperative. Almost at the expense of all else. My love of military history has been on the back burner now for nearly 10 years.

I have also been thrown into association with some of the great contemporary thinkers in Europe and America. So my foray into politics, although brief, has been fruitful for me as a student of libertarianism. Annoying one can never really evolve as anything but a student, because in philosophy - and let us be honest - it is simply a division of that discipline, there is no end solution. Perhaps even suggesting philosophy and discipline together is an oxymoron. Poor student though I am, politics has given me a platform to meet, through the internet, TV, radio and magazines to my certain knowledge more than 60 million people at a rough estimate. Could I have reached them without such a platform? No, I could not possibly have done so. The popular British historians have utilised television to bring millions of people to the subject of history. Fergusson, Starkey, Sharma, Lucy Worsley and many others have opened up a whole field to those without the benefit of a previous formal education.

So we must accept, all of us, that there is no strength as sound or exciting as an idea that has come to its time, some of us must take the traditional path to its promulgation. Every religion requires its disciples. I am uneasy with the laboratory distilled arguments between intellectuals behind closed doors. What I do know is we cannot continue as we are without reversing past the enlightenment into a new dark age. Indeed, it might already be too late.

Defining libertarianism is not simple. Try this one on yourself. Do you like curry? Some of you will, some of you will not. Then if you do, is your preference vindaloo, madras, korma or phal and again chicken, lamb or pork? You see how many variations there are in the answer.

Libertarianism as a philosophy itself branches out into different sub-spheres. Politics, economics, law, mathematics, life styles, who are the prophets of the separate disciplines? How far back do we go to get a broad study started, Milesian? (Pre Socratic) Plato? Aristotle? Do we keep it simple and start with Renaissance Philosophers? Where does science and philosophy cross over? Importantly, what can we learn and whom do we study? Even the newest students of the discipline can name twenty philosophers off the top of their head, if they could not manage their principles, never mind the nuances between those who offer related solutions to modern problems.

I was giving a lecture to the Conservative Association at Cambridge University recently, in other words some of the brightest young minds on the planet. As always in recent years the subject of same sex marriage came up. Surely as a Libertarian I must be in support. How could I not be? As a classical liberal economist and therefore more acutely aware than most of the terror of the economic abyss towards which we lurch and stumble on a daily basis I am always amazed how this question pushes itself to the top. It is interesting as an exercise in debate but really it is akin to being in a burning house with children trapped upstairs and deciding to save the fruit bowl.

One of the audience, I am sure a post-graduate, argued that my conditional response that Robert Nozick would decry my intellectual poltroonery. This is a frequent argument I get from students and the occasional journalist capable of this sort of discussion (oh so few!) that somehow to defeat an argument you take a small aspect to dismantle an intellectually strategic viewpoint. This assumes that to every question there must be an answer, to every problem there must be a solution. Interestingly the people who usually make this sort of deconstructionist argument never apply it to natural science, which is why we suffer climate alarmism hoax.

My reservations on same sex marriage are based on the loss of liberty for the Roman Catholic teacher whom the state insists teaches that same sex marriage has equal validity as traditional. The post-graduate argued that Nozick would not accept that as a reason for failing to support same sex marriage. My counter-argument was that Nozick would, like the Irishman from Kerry 'not start from here'.

This is always the academic dilemma, the Beecher's Brook of theoretical argument. Academics, who by the nature of their profession deal in second hand ideas, spend time guessing how an established philosopher would have interpreted an aspect of modern society beyond their experience, pre or post enlightenment, it makes no difference. The person we should all be trying to liberate is that man in the Leeds Airport Car Park 'Why can't they leave us alone?' He is not interested in Nozick, Schopenhaur, Hegel or indeed anyone else. He wants those chains of which Rousseau speaks but does not understand removed. Nor is academic argument particularly fruitful. Having lectured at universities and schools as a guest for twenty years my experience is the human mind becomes hermetically sealed at the age of twenty-two, which is why the state keeps a relentless death grip on the education of young minds. Governments have long accepted the Jesuit principal of 'give me the boy and I will give you the man'. Politicians and bureaucrats are committed to the status quo if that is what serves their interest.

Where our freedoms have been encroached upon the state apparatus can usually be found to have breached

English law and constitution. This has been allowed to happen for a number of reasons. The judiciary has been politicised. This is how the protection to the constitution has been thwarted; it is almost impossible to take a constitutional issue to the House of Lords, the establishment simply dead hand the process, political pressure chokes off justice at the last fence. The days of the great legal minds have gone, they went with Denning and his ilk. We now have a generation of Englishmen and women without the benefit of a traditional education. The British Prime Minister was a classic example. His staggering ignorance of Magna Carta on American TV shocked viewers there and was hushed up in Britain.

Whenever I talk of Magna Carta, the Tolerance Act, Bill of Rights, 19th Century Reform Bills, Principals of English Law, students stare at me in a bovine sort of way whilst their faculty stares fixedly at the ceiling, equally ignorant.

This is true of the other hijacked democracies of the world, the USA a prime example. US politicians claim Thomas Jefferson could not envisage modern America so the constitution is no longer relevant. Of course Jefferson imagined modern America, only too well which is why the constitution was written thus. It is much easier to steal things from the people if they had no idea they owned them in the first place.

Edward Gibbon recognised this, 'The principles of a free constitution are irrevocably lost when the legislative power is nominated by the executive'.

How can we define libertarianism to my friend in the car park? The man on the Clapham omnibus, Joe Sixpack? Let us move away from the lofty heights of academic debate. Men fought and died in the English

Civil War for the ideal of parliamentary democracy, many of the men without formal education but a deep conviction. I was born in 1949; I have seen huge inroads into personal freedom in my lifetime. My grandfather, an Edwardian gentleman of the old school would not recognise modern Britain. War, as it so often is, to blame. Warfare sees the enormous theft of freedom by a centralised state for the common good. Freedoms are never returned. It is always about money and power, taxation, political or bureaucratic office.

So can an individual regain control of his life, indeed his soul? Can he wrest it from the state which has permeated his body, gradually, relentlessly and without his understanding? Can we rescue that poor bewildered individual in the Leeds Airport car park? 'Why don't they leave us alone?' Let us look at how 'they' do it. To understand the enemy is half-way to defeating him.

Chapter 2

Politics, Journalists and Pavlov's Dog

It was, I think, P J O'Rourke who claimed that politics is show business for ugly people. It is obviously true whomsoever coined the phrase. Politicians and journalists need each other; like actors and critics they are the flip side of the same coin. Neither all politicians nor journalists are exactly the same, any more than horses or dogs. They are a species and break down into breeds and many if not all carry similar characteristics. Alsatians, Pekinese, Jack Russells and Border Collies are all dogs, and there it ends, but few readers will need guidance on their physical or personality differences.

The journalist is no different; there are many breeds and as they hold themselves protectors of democracy, the citizen, the unfairly dealt with, the environment etc, etc, they are of course nothing of the sort. They are the establishment. They are 'they'. It is vital to understand this if any counter-revolution against the mighty establishment of the state is to be mounted. They come in different guises. I deliberately leave out in this chapter the local journalist. He is generally underpaid, under-resourced, diligent, trustworthy and honourable, came to and remains in journalism from conviction and a genuine desire to add value to the community in which he serves. His editor panders to the establishment often because he has no choice. He survives by revenue and sales, his paper does not survive because it is owned by a billionaire who offers huge subsidies with political or commercial ambitions disconnected with journalism. Ownership of a national newspaper is often for the same personal satisfaction that magnates own football clubs. After all, if you have made your billions, have your Learjet and yacht festooned with trophy women and champagne, bought your island retreat, you are kicking around for something to spend the loot on. In days of yore it would be philanthropy. The Nuffields, Carneigies and Gettys sought the ticket to slide past St Peter into the member's enclosure. And why not?

The twenty first century oligarch buys a newspaper. It has been this way since newspapers started, arguably from when The Times was a serious newspaper and known affectionately as the Thunderer. The historian might suggest the early days of the Manchester Guardian were more altruistic and who am I to argue?

The Editor, given ownership criteria and political influence is barely worth a mention. He is told what to think and what and whom to support. Owners never interfere with editorial policy, perish the thought! However, they are pretty soon packing their bags if they transgress. This is relatively rare as the selection procedure is pretty thorough. Most national papers hail straight from the comically corrupt and drunken Eatonswill election, described in Dickens's Pickwick Papers, held before the electoral reforms of the later 19th Century. If the reader wants an amusing lesson of how newspapers behave at election time, dig out a copy. 150 years old, but the same today as it ever was. Indeed, nowadays most editorials in the Conservative supporting papers, i.e. nearly all of them, seem to have their editorials written by Conservative Party central office. They are traditionally unsigned but the writing style is unmistakeable and they are 'party' political as opposed to political. There are no radical editors of any national newspaper today in the United Kingdom, nor have there been arguably since the war. The Honours system helps this cosy alliance. In brief, House of Lords for the proprietor, Knighthood for the Editor, triples all round as Private Eye would say. Incidentally every bit a part of the establishment today as the Spectator, only printed on poor quality paper to give it a radical appearance.

Another breed, not in their order of importance, indeed if there is one, is the features journalist. They have more in common with the local journalist, usually the best of breed, write much better quality English, take far more trouble, do much more research and put in far more shoe leather than their colleagues, with the possible exception, ironically of the sports writers. The features editor actually cares about quality and content, regardless of the paper. One suspects their work is archived personally. They believe their pieces will stand the test of time and I suspect they are right.

Enter then the economics editor. Like the curate's egg they are 'good in parts'. We will all have our favourite who has a track record awesome in its misunderstanding of the modern world of mercantilism and crony capitalism. As always when one is wrong on a scale a broken clock could only dream of, reward is good and swift. No not the sack, but an academic appointment or seat in the House of Lords. Being 100% wrong is a much clearer and more useful guide to decision-making for the reader than being seventy five percent right like myself. There have been in recent years a few genuinely good economics editors, Liam Halligan and Alistair Heath.

But the true master/mistress of the breed is the political journalist. I leave aside here the sketch writer, largely because I stopped reading them since Frank Johnson retired from it, a bit like moving from hand-pulled real ale to Heineken, although I am sure there are some good ones around.

I mean the right on, no holds barred journeyman reporter. This is both man and dog, and the dog is Pavlov's. These wonderful characters are bound with hoops of steel to the world of political correctness. They have a lexicon with which they share with their brethren in broadcasting. Without this Achilles Heel, (don'tcha just luv a mixed metaphor?) they would be almost impossible to manipulate from the bottom end of back bench politics. Everything for them is 'today'. They must file their copy by tonight, very few have had the benefit of a traditional education, they might have a university degree although this is not of primary importance. What fascinates is their complete lack of original thought. Any proposal of libertarian values and they are quite genuinely shocked. Because their paper, right or left, is deeply committed to the status quo, any alternative is considered blasphemous. I honestly tried to find another word. As a libertarian I devote the next few pages to scrupulously documented anecdotes to leave the reader to make their own assessment. To understand how political thought is successfully manipulated is an essential chapter for the bewildered and frustrated citizen.

The Times newspaper did an interview with me in which I took a view on morality and politics. This was 7 years after my lawyers elicited a full retraction and apology in an allegation I used prostitutes from the BBC. 'Strange Mr Bloom takes a moral view when he admits to visiting prostitutes.' Yes, I got right of reply but to what end? Bloom's letter to The Times 'I do not, nor have I ever used the service of prostitutes.' Not very convincing is it? Especially as I am a known advocate of legalisation. All one does is blow up the story.

Another interviewer, a significantly more intelligent and diligent lady sought my view on a supposed libertarian dilemma. Would not under your system allow a pub landlord to put a notice in the window of his pub 'No Blacks'. Notice not the suggestion of a black publican putting a notice in the window 'No Whites', or indeed 'No Gays'. Yet any libertarian having read Janet and John Book I on the subject knows that discretion on to who enters your house or place of business is a fundamental pillar of the creed. No black, white, gay or anyone else is harmed by such freedom of association because there is always somewhere else to go where the spirit of commerce is more entrepreneurial. Very, very few business people turn away custom from whomsoever it is offered. I might take a different view if there was an incitement to violence in the advertised message. I am sure that those readers with a broader experience of the real world will know that it is far more likely a non-gay is excluded from a gay club, bar or hostel than vice versa. There are haunts in London, Manchester and New York where no white face would dare to go.

Another piece of gratuitous unpleasantness was in the Daily Telegraph by an occasional political observer. There is a big bold picture of my father in my autobiography 'Guinea a Minute'. In the uniform of a Royal Air Force Officer, wings on display and North Africa Star. There is also a photograph of him as a senior conservative with Prime Minister Harold Macmillan as a London Councillor and City businessman. The journalist, in a completely unrelated aside, referred to me as the 'son of a Lewisham gas fitter'. Appalling snobbery, my increasing popularity with his readers had to be dealt with. By implication pretend to his conservative middle-class readership I was not of their kidney, so any fellow feeling they might have entertained was curtailed. How patronising of his readers, what brings people like him into journalism?

Another bizarre incident, again with the BBC during the 2009 Euro elections, they invited me to the Leeds studio 24 hours before the election. The first time in the entire campaign they wanted to talk to me, although I was the incumbent up for re-election. I go to the studio at some inconvenience, I was on the other side of the constituency. First question 'Do you employ your niece on your secretarial allowance?' This in the style of a leading Queen's Council cross-examining a suspected child molester. My wife's niece at the time worked for me two days a week; she is a fully qualified secretary from a prestigious London secretarial school. 'Er, yes' I said, 'and your point being?' Ah ha! Gotcha was the response. Why should I not? The implication was I had been found out doing something illegal. Shall we talk about the campaign, the issues I suggested? No! End of interview. Yet all the establishment MEPs had their spouses on their allowances, one for £50,000 per year for very spurious and vague reasons. But you see they were establishment.

But the point is, none of this works. People are not as stupid as the press or media would have you believe. Abuse and vilification are easily seen through. I was re-elected with an increased majority. Letters of support rolled in again. The British always support the underdog. Every time they do it, more invitations to speak pour in.

To paraphrase therefore Oscar Wilde, "There is only one thing worse than being vilified, it is not being vilified."

I once had a Chief Executive who in most regards was pretty useless, but he did teach me one good thing, 'Never give examples of one'. I therefore take some time and trouble to go into some depth on how press and media deliberately misquote, take out of context, spin or twist any idea which is perceived to be anti-establishment, i.e. anti 'them' by proxy. Before I do so, let me make it perfectly clear I believe in a free press, unregulated, only bound by common decency, courtesy and modest libel laws. Anyone who goes into politics must understand when you stand for public office you are no longer, in the modern world, entitled to be treated as an ordinary citizen. There is no more point in complaining about it than complaining of bruises on the rugby field or in the boxing ring or the dodgy LBW decision at cricket. In many ways it is a shame because it keeps good and able people out of politics. Enoch Powell suggested a politician complaining about journalists was like a bit like a farmer complaining about the weather. Look at the choice great nations produce at election time the UK, USA, France and Italy and ask yourself are they the best people available? Of course not, they are the only people prepared to apply for the job.

Let me review just a few instances over the last ten years to show how the anti-establishment politician is subject to a systematic attack, not all of which succeed and indeed many back-fire.

In 2004, on the day I took office in Strasbourg I joined the Women's Rights and Gender Equality Committee. Probably the silliest committee in the 'parliament', which is saying something, but no matter. Under European employment law the game is so stacked against the employer, particularly small businesses, that young women often are discriminated against because of draconian maternity leave laws. There are literally thousands of words on this subject on the UK government's website; it is an impenetrable maze for the layman, i.e. small business proprietor, in England incidentally many of whom are women. Not only does a woman not have to divulge she is pregnant at interview, if she decides to have a baby she does not have to commit to returning until very late in the leave period. The business therefore struggles to cover for her and cannot commit to a new full-time employee. Employers covertly discriminate in favour of the employee whose children are grown up. Can you believe it is also illegal to even ask a young woman what her family plans might be? When I was interviewed by the press I explained that no small businessman with his brain in the right place would submit to such nonsense. There was forty-eight hours of the most extraordinary press hysteria. My experience is only truth can produce such a reaction in the press. Honest, blunt Yorkshire businessmen came up to me at conferences to wonder how a statement of the blindingly obvious could cause such a reaction. I was 'Neanderthal', a 'dinosaur', 'mad', a 'misogynist, 'sexist' and 'anti-women'. My quite legitimate point was that the legislation actually disadvantaged young women. Repeal it and watch more of them recruited to small businesses which represent 80% of the UK economy. By the end of the week the Sunday newspapers realised I had touched a nerve with ordinary working people and the whole emphasis changed and a debate on the unintended consequences of employment law went national. The whole object of my initial response. In a completely different and private conversation I joked that women did not clean behind the fridge. Quite unconnected with maternity legislation and taken as an obvious joke at the time.

However, since that day it has been impossible for any debate at any university or on TV or radio for me not to be quoted as follows "Women should not work, they should stay at home and clean behind the fridge!" This absurd nonsense was spouted by a TUC 'Wimmin's Spokesperson' on radio last year and she had to suffer the humiliation of my £1,000 offer to charity if she could produce the transcript or any evidence of this 'quote'. When papers have a misquote they re-quote it ad nauseum until it becomes a cliché and joins the

'Play it again Sam' popular lines which were never actually said.

The following year the press overstepped the mark and claimed I had 'groped' a student in Brussels. Now this is a different game altogether. The reporter from a well-known popular paper knew the story was untrue. The 'incident' was supposed to have taken place in a public restaurant with 100 guests, many of whom were journalists. My wife was present, the student was at a separate table and turned out later to be a gate-crashing, socialist worker member. There was a petition signed by all the other students that it was a lie and she was an imposter and moreover all this was known by the reporter. But the paper was a bastion of the Conservative Party, ironic? And it was a simple smear. Now in spite of all this evidence it took five weeks and £10,000 in legal fees to get a complete retraction and full apology via the press complaints agency. I should have sued for a large sum of money but I wanted the story killed as soon as possible. The reporter left soon afterwards but has popped up at The Independent large as life with no contrition or humility. What draws such people into journalism one wonders?

In the course of my career I have been asked to enter the debate on prostitution. As a libertarian I always argue that the worst possible idea is to make it illegal. Dangerous and wrong. The BBC interviewed me for half an hour in York on the subject and assured me it was a serious and important debate. We ranged from illegal immigration to cultural differences across the world. I explained the Hong Kong business cultural background, Japan, and differences with London and New York. One question was, had I in my Far East business days, visited brothels? No, but certainly I had visited the girlie bars in the Wan Chai district of Hong Kong after a 'night out with the lads'. Pretty harmless stuff, in London you wobble off for a curry. The interviewer went straight into the market square and told passers-by, 'your MEP has admitted visiting brothels. What do you think?' They then interviewed live a member of the opposition who said I was 'that sort of man, who disrespects women'. My lawyers rousted out the producer of the programme and the next night it started with an unreserved apology for misleading the public. This is public service broadcasting, not a tabloid. The same public service broadcasters who, when I made a joke about 'sluts', invaded my little Yorkshire village, knocked on every door to try and find someone to say something nasty about me on air. No one would talk to them so they went fifty miles to another town and misled three completely bewildered strangers who had clearly never heard of me, into suggesting I should resign.

More recently still, I exposed the scandal of the UK government sending £1 billion per month abroad in so-called Foreign Aid when the country is borrowing £9 billion per month and closing hospitals, cutting defence, police and other public services and raising taxes. Most of the money is wasted even if it can be accounted for, which is not often.

This is where the wonderful Pavlov's Dog response can be relied upon. Such is the world of political correctness in the lexicon of the nation's press and media it is always possible to get a subject onto the front burner if you do not mind a bit of personal vilification. For two years I had been making speeches about this immoral scam to no avail. Frustrated I gazed into the camera lens in Birmingham in a speech on economics and suggested we were mad to be sending money to 'Bongo Bongo Land'. It took them four weeks, but the press were up in arms about me as a racist and baby killer. God! They are so easy to wind up, like a clockwork toy. My debate was launched at last. It took only hours before the press and media realised they had misjudged the mood of the nation again. Tens of thousands of phone calls and emails flooded into newspapers, TV and radio shows across the nation. Awesome. The most successful political speech I had made up to that point. Although by no means the last. My old party, UKIP, languishing on 14% in the polls and sliding, went up to 20% and membership applications locally shot through the roof. I received private letters from some of the most senior business people in the country. I was sent a set of Bongo drums from Scotland, a barrel of beer named Bongo juice from a local brewer and filled my diary up for 6 months with speaking engagements. My niece got VIP status in a local night club called the Bongo Club. Strangers in pubs came up to talk to me and buy me a beer. So I was glad I took no notice on Nigel Farage's instruction to apologise. Unlike Nigel, I paid attention in geography lessons so I knew there was no such place as Bongo Bongo land so there was no-one to whom I could apologise.

Such is the sealed world now of the London journalist they have got completely out of touch with what ordinary working folk think. Now that has died down, not the debate incidentally which remains and will remain on the front burner, the papers have reverted to me being in disgrace about the use of the term. National newspapers who vilified me are now leading the campaign to stop the overseas aid swindle. No mention of me of course but I can reflect over the years that I have made some small impact on behalf of the downtrodden and abused electorate.

What does the libertarian deduce from this chapter? May I suggest that such is the fear generated by the libertarian, so difficult to refute in rational argument abuse and vilification is the sole weapon of the establishment.

I could, after ten years continue to cite hundreds more examples but I wind up with just a few. In the Sheffield Star there was an Op-Ed on me personally about 600 words and carried a picture. It was, as usual, completely hostile. I had never heard of the journalist, he had never met me or spoken to me on the telephone, yet he felt qualified to write a significant piece with me as the subject.

I spoke at the Oxford Union where every speaker had a pop at me personally, I retaliated only once to an undergraduate speaker with a pretty barbed comment. I was vilified then by Douglas Murray of the Spectator and other journalists for so doing, implying I had caused 'offence'; there is that word again. Yet Murray stood a few feet away from me at the post debate party which lasted until 1.00 am where it was abundantly clear no 'offence' had been taken. The undergrad in question invited me to go on to a club along with his chums. No mention of course of this or the picture taken with him at his request. I was invited to speak again at the union only ten weeks later.

A few weeks later I spoke at Cambridge University, a lecture on economics, forty minutes and questions. The Cambridge News deliberately misquoted me and suggested Cambridge should 'save money' by not inviting me again. I paid for my own train journey, dinner and hotel. But no matter when vilification is the order of the day.

For twenty years I have been one of the leading sponsors (as a businessman) of women's sport equestrianism and rugby. I have donated most of my attendance allowances over and above expenses to British charities for over 10 years. None of this has ever been reported in any newspaper. Not once, ever. The Asian Age referred to me as a clown, yet I am received with great hospitality and warmth by all my Asian constituents and have visited their holy places in the Indian sub-continent. The reporter (Mr Dhondy) has never bothered to make contact with me. So the list grows; I make no mention of the rather silly young women who write for the tabloids to whom I seem irresistible to vilify whenever they need to file a bit of copy.

Matthew D'Ancona, a Tory Party journeyman hack wrote an editorial piece in the Sunday Telegraph, needless to say more inaccurate denigration. I wrote to the then editor, Patience Wheatcroft for right of reply. Just a short letter and I was refused. This is completely against quality newspaper protocol. The Western Morning News consistently refers to me in a derogatory manner. No right of reply even after three separate occasions and many phone calls and emails.

The most recent example, the Daily Telegraph reported me with a 'quote' on the UKIP leadership. The article was by a chap called James Kirkup. Never met him, never talked to him. The 'quote' was completely fictitious but it is the Telegraph, ergo it must be true.

Again, let me make it very clear it matters not to me. I speak always to full houses. Standing room only wherever I go. Does the 'man on the Clapham Omnibus' believe any of this nonsense? Not really; people are not as stupid as the press seems to think. This is why they are dying. It is a shame because newspapers still have so much to offer, perhaps more so now than ever. They can only survive with serious opinion and accurate reporting. Paradoxically it is my most hostile political press foe, The Guardian, where you will find the most accurate and researched news and opinion. They always pay me the courtesy of a telephone call before they have a pop.

I looked through some past transcripts of TV and radio interviews in order that they might provide a guide to the establishment technique. I know not if the questions are motivated by an establishment political viewpoint or simply just stupid. I suspect a bit of both. The experienced libertarian interviewee will be totally familiar with this but the newcomer might find it interesting and perhaps even amusing. These are in no particular order of importance, just a random selection.

Subject: Decriminalisation of drugs

There can be no doubt, nor have I ever heard any intelligent person not agree, that current international policy has failed. Drugs are more easily available to children in my constituency than cigarettes and they are cheaper. Police and prison budgets are squeezed dry by prohibition. There has been much work done by libertarians on this subject and I do not intend to make the arguments here. The establishment has decided prohibition is the permanent policy so no new thought is allowed. Indeed, debate is heavily suppressed.

Everyone's elderly relatives therefore remain at risk from addicts crazed in pursuit of drug money. Old people were never attacked fifty years ago. It simply did not happen. It is now commonplace.

It is a directly drug related hideous crime. Yet the interview will always follow thus,

"So, Mr Bloom, you want to decriminalise drugs? Even hard drugs?"

"Yes".

"Do you have children?"

You can see the inference at once. Somehow decriminalisation will lead to a mass take up of across the counter drugs. The follow-up will be,

"Have you seen the havoc drug addiction can wreak?"

The inference I simply do not care.

The establishment politician "Mr Bloom is criminally irresponsible for suggesting this". This passes for debate, even on the occasion it is allowed to take place. Where are the in-depth programmes analysing the thousands of billions of dollars spent pursuing the failing policy of prohibition? Why do people assume children, even their own, would become addicted to drugs if they were available across the counter? How is it that they cannot see amongst certain social groups the take up of cigarettes is as high as it ever was, yet the better educated social groups have almost completely eradicated addiction to tobacco. Pretty clear to any rational observer that addiction to drugs, and I include alcohol and tobacco is linked to education, motivation and peer pressure. I absolve David Aaronovitch from this attitude as one of the few senior journalists to speak out.

Subject: Education

Consider if you will, home education. Many responsible parents cannot afford private education but do not want to expose their precious offspring to the local sink school where their values are disregarded. Believe me, I have first-hand experience in my constituency of these heart-breaking problems.

"You believe in home education, Mr Bloom, but if it was not closely regulated and monitored how can you be sure parents will act responsibly?"

The implication here is somehow the state cares more about a child than its parents. That the establishment with its own agenda somehow would work better for the child's interests. In spite of all the blindingly obvious failings in the Anglosphere of failing state education somehow anything is better than the parents. That one rogue parent in a thousand or ten thousand is a reason to hamper the concept. The precautionary principle. I will return to that in another chapter.

Subject: Minimum Wage

Most western European nations have a minimum wage. A disastrous policy for young people. Youth unemployment ranges from 30% to 50%. A minimum wage prices the unskilled out of the job market, they cannot get on the employment ladder. Germany is the exception with only 9%. The only major economy not to have a minimum wage. Here is how the interview goes with the Good Morning Britain tele-prompted sofa moron presenter.

"So, Mr Bloom, you do not believe in a minimum wage? Won't this lead to exploitation of people by employers?"

"No" (I outline the facts just mentioned).
Miss Teleprompt "Would you work for £9 an hour?"
This passes for debate in sound bite land.

Subject: Racism

Let us look at how the establishment deal with racism. This particular 'ism' is extremely ephemeral, yet the draconian law that goes with it is not. What does it mean? Well, in the memorable words penned by the estimable observer of human character Lewis Carol, "What is racism? It is whatever the establishment, media or political opposition want it to mean". Let me pick up on my now very well-known speech on the economy in Birmingham. A forty minute speech as referred to in another chapter during which I exposed the scandal of £1 billion per month in largely unaudited foreign aid. (Incidentally that is 50% of 2018 UK GDP growth!)

A Channel 4 interviewer (for overseas readers this channel is state sponsored with highly left-wing establishment presenters with well-known past socialist political affiliations).

"Mr Bloom, who or what did you mean by Bongo Bongo Land?"

"I meant it as a euphemism for a tin pot dictatorship, a country non-democratic and contemptuous of its own people".

"Did you mean Africa?"

"It could be anywhere, a bit like Banana Republic but that is not the point; I am here to discuss the appalling scam where we send £1 billion per month when we are closing our hospitals."

"I don't want to talk about that; I want to talk about what many people believe to be an offensive and racist remark".

"Who could it offend? There is no such place as Bongo Bongo Land, so it cannot possibly offend anyone. Can we move on to the real debate now, please".

"No, I don't want to move on. I want to talk about your racist attitude".

"Can we move on?"

"No".

"Then I am terminating the interview".

"You are giving up?"

"Well, yes, there is no point in continuing it for either of us, is there?"

The interviewer, Krishnan Guru-Murthy, was clearly terrified of the debate moving on to what people really wanted to hear.

I was interviewed by him several years ago on maternity leave. My usual point that it deters women from being offered jobs with small businesses.

"So, Mr Bloom, you do not believe married women should work?"

"How on earth could you deduce that? I want the very opposite, I want to make it easier for them to get work".

"You do realise half the population are women?"

"Your point being?"

"Well, they won't be voting for you, will they?"

"I have enormous support for this initiative, many from businesswomen who completely agree with me".

"Do you know any young women, Mr Bloom?"

The inference here is I am too old, too much of a dinosaur not just to have a view on maternity legislation but to even know any young women! You might enjoy my last word,

"What is the selection procedure to become a London ITV interviewer?"

You get the drift though. I have other examples too numerous to mention. The inference is always, you are either mad, eccentric, out of touch, too old, fill in the gaps. Never at any stage is an answer discussed or challenged; there is then the cut back to the anchorman. This is always a really subtle ploy. The slightly raised eyebrow, the almost, but not quite imperceptible shrugs, the momentarily lifted eyes to the ceiling. Then the move the 'independent' panel of assessors from the 'disinterested' press. Always an array of left-wing fake iconoclastic journalists who are steeped in political correctness and deeply connected to the establishment. Check out who owns their papers and magazines. One delicious example on me from Helen Lewis of the New Statesman.

"I know Mr Bloom is sexist because he tries to refute it by having random pictures of himself with women". The only pictures you will find are of my association going back 20 years sponsoring women's sport. Rugby and Equestrianism in the main and of course with my many female colleagues of long standing.

All this is fairly standard procedure. Every TV and radio show, every magazine and newspaper represents the establishment. Left, right or centre of politics is not relevant at all because they are just different departments of the establishment, dependent on the status quo. This is why no-one votes anymore. The man on the 'Clapham Omnibus' gets it, as does Joe Sixpack across the pond. They just do not know how to change it.

How can it be therefore that I generate hostility from the establishment and approbation from the electorate in equal measure? My speeches in the EU 'Parliament' are the most viewed by any politician in that establishment's history. May I suggest that libertarianism is far more popular amongst people than previously imagined, that government are beginning to take fright? Why, indeed, can they not leave us alone?

Another fascinating insight into the institutional establishment mind set is yet again provided by the BBC. A features television programme with a fairly good reputation asked if they could accompany me to Strasbourg and 'shadow' me throughout a 'parliamentary' plenary session. The guest interviewer was heavy-weight boxer Johnny Nelson, a man of great character and humour. Throughout six days he was with me asking questions in my village, in my office and in the city of Strasbourg. By this stage I was quite an experienced interviewee. Throughout the six days Johnny asked me, I suppose, about twenty relevant, pertinent and succinct questions. The producer knew her business and the three of us formed a good, friendly and workmanlike relationship. As always with these programmes several days and miles of film go to make but 15 minutes of documentary time. I understand this, I have been at it long enough. My friends and I, indeed half the county sat down on the Monday evening to watch it. Stunningly, amazingly, every single question had been edited out. I do not mean half, or even three quarters. I mean every single one. In my opinion, the editor had turned it into a bad travelogue of Strasbourg. It had been edited into a meaningless shamble. It was not hostile, it was not anything. It was a complete and utter waste of everyone's resources. What was worse, I thought it effectively terminated what could have been a very interesting second career for Johnny Nelson. A lovely, bright and articulate man, a great advert for sportsmen and boxing in particular. To my mind, the editing made him look incompetent. I learned yet another lesson about the establishment and in particular the BBC. No matter how sympathetic the people on the front team of a programme are, biased editorial will kill it. At the time of writing, the BBC Chairman is in receipt of a fat EU pension and the institution regularly borrows money from the European Investment Bank interest free. It seems that the Eurosceptic, classical liberal libertarian will be poisoned by editorship at every opportunity.

I recently did a light-hearted news/comedy panel show. The panellists were all witty, amusing and trendy TV celebs. They all knew each other, go to the same parties and were tremendously pleased with themselves. They are professional fake anti-establishment talking heads. Of course, should you get the best of the exchange the editor steps forward with the scissors. You are there to be pilloried not to look as clever and as witty as them. Close examination showed even the crudeness of it. Friends asked me why I suddenly choked off a response. Did I have a frog in my throat? Scissors, old fashioned but still very useful to the not quite so clever establishment panellist.

Chapter 3

Why We Cannot Trust Government Statistics

To paraphrase Joseph Addison, governments put me in mind of the scuttle fish, when he is unable to extricate himself blackens all the water about him until he becomes invisible.

They are always trying to convince us that things are better than we feel in our bones that they actually are. Why is this? The obvious answer, and one that is true as far as it goes, is that government wants us to re-elect the incumbents. The current administration simply wants to keep its jobs. Slogans such as "You've never had it so good" are combined with patriotic theatre to make us feel good about our current batch of government parasites and vote to keep them in office. This kind of "feel good about us, so we can keep our jobs" goes on everywhere, not just in government. "Buy locally from your hometown", "fill-in-the-blank". "Our business has the friendliest employees". However, in business, if you reported false sales numbers to your boss or false profit numbers to stockholders, you would lose your job and possibly go to gaol. But falsifying economic statistics in order to keep a government job has been honed to a fine art, and yet no one loses his job and no one goes to gaol.

There is something much more serious and much more frightening going on that moves government to falsify economic statistics. Government is full of megalomaniacs, both elected and appointed, who desire POWER. Lord Acton's warning to Englishmen that "Power corrupts and absolute power corrupts absolutely" was matched by Abraham Lincoln in his earliest important address, delivered to the Young Men's Lyceum of Springfield, Illinois in 1837.

In this address Lincoln observed that the days of heroes were over for America. The separation from the Mother Country was secure and the federalist form of government was accepted throughout the Union. The real threat to America would come internally, from ambitious men who did not desire to labour at the mundane machinery of everyday government but who wished to perform great deeds while at the helm of the coercive power of the state. Lincoln gave us an early warning of the end-of-the-century Progressive Movement. These ambitious men desired power over money and liberties in order to carry out their fervently held, messianic visions of the perfect society here on earth. Ironically Lincoln joined their ranks in 1860. We shall return shortly to these twin avenues to power; i.e., control of money and limitations on our liberties.

Now, in the private sphere, this desire for power is benign. In the private sphere we choose to follow men of our own volition. We may tolerate nasty bosses because we are well paid or recognise their personal faults as irrelevant to the success of our professional careers. Likewise, we may turn a blind eye to the off-field antics of members of our favourite sports teams or our favourite celebrities. But these men have no real power over us. We can always leave our job and work for someone else, and we can always give our allegiance to another. Not so in the public sphere, where personal faults are now tolerated by a disillusioned public.

We return now to control of money and suppression of our liberties, those twin avenues by which parasites and megalomaniacs maintain their POWER. Libertarians understand that money is as much a part of the private capitalist market as any other good or service. There is absolutely no need for government control of money. During America's and the UK's greatest period of growth (and what was probably the greatest period of growth by any two nations in history), from the early 1860's until the start of the First World War in 1914, America did not have a central bank or a central money-issuing authority. Regulation of business and personal liberty was almost non-existent. There were no drug laws or required licenses for starting most businesses. There was no federal income tax! Internal excise taxes and external tariffs funded what little government Americans needed. Post Napoleonic European growth similarly was unprecedented. Gold was money, there was no government-owned central bank.

How could the power-hungry politicians and bureaucrats break out of this natural limitation on their megalomaniacal designs? First, they convinced the world that only a government could issue money and only through a central bank, controlled of course by the government itself. It then proceeded to print more and more money to fund its grand designs. But there was a flaw in their plan - money printing caused boom/bust recessions. The new money masqueraded as real, sound money and enticed entrepreneurs and capitalists to begin long-term projects for which there were insufficient resources for their profitable completion. How to solve this problem? Convince the public that the very problems caused by money printing can only be solved by coercive regulations designed by these same power-hungry politicians and their sycophantic bureaucrats. But reality has a nasty way of thwarting these plans, as people sense that all is not well. Businesses seem to be closing or not expanding as expected. Unemployment seems to be rising and wages stagnate for the still employed. How to fool the people into not believing their very eyes. Enter the government statistician. Does the Consumer Price Index reveal price inflation? No problem. Just stop counting some every day, necessary items, such as energy and food. Is the official unemployment statistic rising? No problem. Just stop counting those long-term unemployed who have become so discouraged that they have ceased looking for work. Convince the sycophantic, Big Government-loving media to repeat and repeat the myth that prices are not rising and unemployment is falling. Above all, introduce more programmes to funnel money to favoured constituents and vilify political opponents as causing the problem. This works especially well when vilifying bankers. Convince the public that bankers who fail must be saved by the taxpayer because the world will end if they are allowed to go under.

Keynesian school economics dovetails nicely with all this nonsense. Savings is scorned and spending is celebrated. And if the public will not spend enough to achieve full employment, the government must do it for them with printed money. Oh, the wonders of Keynesianism that turns profligacy into a virtue! Now throw into the mix the concept of Gross Domestic Product (GDP). GDP is the sum total of all (mostly) consumer spending. According to Keynesian orthodoxy, the higher the GDP the better the economy. Spending, not savings, is the key to this fallacy. Now we find government pursuing an inflationary policy in order to pump up the GDP numbers and convince the gullible public that they really are better off than they feel and would be worse off without their benevolent government saviours. Here is an example. The number of gallons of petrol sold each month in America changed little from the first summer of President Obama's administration in 2009 until the same month in 2013, yet petrol prices doubled from around $1.80 to around $3.50 per gallon. Now, most people would say that if you are consuming the same volume of a product, you really have not increased your well-being from this product. Yet, because GDP is the aggregate of total dollar sales, that part of the economy measured by gasoline sales double! Here's another one: there is a movement in Europe to add to GDP what has always been private services from one family member to another, such as caring for an aged parent. Adding the so-called monetary worth of these private services will boost GDP and make the party in power appear to have performed an economic miracle! All western industrial democratic governments play this game.

All of this manipulation of employment and GDP statistics is geared at one thing - convince the public that the political control over money, which leads to coercive control over individuals and the economy by power hungry statists, is working wonders. Add to this propaganda the threat that any cutback in government spending would force politicians to close down the national health, suspend police and firemen, stop old age pensions etc. and the public falls quickly into line.

Chapter 4

Everything the state does is inept or incompetent.

How can we release our friend in the Leeds car park from his shackles? The relative freedom of the United Kingdom has all but disappeared in my lifetime. We have suffered more legislation in the last twenty-five years than in the entire period from 1688 to 1997, most of this is the result of subcontracting law to the European Union and its prescriptive judicial system. We are now told that which we may do, not that which we may not. Such legislation is enforced by agencies empowered by enabling legislation. The principles of English law are now set aside, adjudication is behind closed doors by journeymen bureaucrats in our everyday dealings with the state. The motorist is particularly vulnerable, hence a separate chapter.

How did we get where we are? When did we abandon a three hundred and fifty year old principle established by Sir Edward Coke that an 'Englishman's home is his castle'? When was the concept of natural justice, as understood by the man on the Clapham Omnibus, forsaken? We know that war is the thief of justice, not only truth. The state confiscates freedoms for the supposedly common good and, of course, only temporarily. But the state is incapable of returning power to the citizen. It has no machinery to do so. Moreover, the politician and

bureaucrat is of a genre; they genuinely believe they are necessary and act in the best interest of the citizen. Their experience of life is astonishingly limited, hence their addiction to what Austrian economists understand as the 'fatal conceit'. That they and they alone are qualified to decide on any and every issue of the day and their remit is without limit. Google if you will, maternity law, paternity law, employment law on holidays, working hours, pensions, conditions of work. For enlightenment on how absurd has become our world also try bananas, duck eggs, tractor seats, spirit bottles, MOT certification. In fact, Google anything and you will find government or quango involvement.

Even insurance underwriting is not exempt. Young women pay more for their motor insurance and retiring men are disadvantaged with annuity purchase under EU regulation. Government pressure is exerted to make insurance companies accept flood risk against the principles of free underwriting. Supermarkets are intimidated into removing chocolate from checkout points or marketing buy one and get one free. My own club was forced by law to close our beautiful ladies' drawing room and I cannot enjoy a cigar after dinner without standing outside. Those of the Orthodox Christian faith fear arrest or intimidation for expressing sincerely held views on the interpretation of the bible. The list is quite literally endless. When I was a boy you would often hear the phrase 'it is a free country'. I have not heard it for thirty years; indeed most would laugh or scoff if you used it. It now would be patently absurd.

Philosophers over the ages have abhorred this encroachment by government. From the ancient Greeks to Hoppe and Rothbard whose conviction is that limited government is unachievable. I have not yet reached this uncompromising position, albeit I sympathise slightly more with it as each day goes by.

Everything the state does is inept or incompetent. This is true of all western industrial democracies. People strive desperately to make enough money to extract themselves from the state system. Private health plans flourish, anything but an NHS hospital! Ordinary families beggar themselves to pay private education fees, public transport is the last resort, the Town Hall is a bonfire for money. Yet after seventy years of peace, tax and national debt has never been higher. One wonders how much worse it could be if we returned to an absolute monarchy, even the Stuarts were not as incompetent as government post 1914.

How can Great Britain return, not to former glory, but to modest competence for which most of us would settle?

Obviously electoral reform; I have covered this elsewhere, but basically no representation without taxation. If you do not contribute you cannot expect to be granted a view on expenditure. In short if you do not put into 'the whip' you do not get a beer. But most important the education system needs a complete overhaul. I probably speak at more schools and universities than most elected politicians from the senior chambers of government.

Young people are simply not being educated. They are going through a carefully controlled government programme of box ticking. GCSEs, A-Levels and University Degrees are a system of stepping stones to get a job. Nothing wrong with that, but any interview with a recent graduate exposes a woeful lack of knowledge or even original thought.

I have found far more encouraging young minds in emerging economies than in the mature industrial democracies. This cannot be a coincidence. As a regular speaker on economics the standard of tutelage in British Universities is embarrassingly bad. History is taught in a sort of vacuum; how can it be possible to ask an undergraduate for essays on the British Reform Acts without a knowledge of the French Revolution or the British Civil War? There is no concept of historical chronological order, without which history becomes a meaningless potpourri of short stories.

No wonder the more exclusive investment houses take their pick from mathematicians, physicists or classicists. I would not touch an economics graduate with a barge pole. It would take too long to un-train them.

Schools must teach the principles of English Law. The state relies on ignorance of the population to facilitate their theft of citizens' birthrights. Look at the pressure on trial by jury, the presumption of innocence, prima facie evidence, habeus corpus, double jeopardy.

I go further, press and broadcasters must learn a new phrase. "Is this the role of government?" Every encroachment should be challenged. This is difficult with public service broadcasting committed by design to the furtherance of state interference. Editors must accept responsibility for their primary role as a protector of truth and first defence from government dictatorship. This is pure Adam Smith mutual self-interest. The reason circulation of newspapers has plummeted is they offer no enlightenment. They are just tools of the main political parties. It seemed for a while, social media would disseminate truth and alternative comment but sadly, government has clamped down on blogs,

Facebook, Twitter and other mediums by the use of new thought crimes, the definition of which is vague but penalties severe.

Covert censorship is rife. I have been visited by police for pretty innocuous tweets and spent ten years try to get Wikipedia to remove lies and half-truths posted by political enemies. To no avail: most people have no idea Wikipedia is politically edited.

If you don't believe me, try posting anything sceptical about global warming.

The most recent coercion is 'climate change' a classic tax and control system - again 'for our own good!'

The story told by environmentalists is that climate change will produce catastrophic consequences, therefore something must be done. Terrible storms will rip our homes from their foundations. Drought will render the land infertile. And endless rains will wash whatever remains of our civilisation into the sea, or drown us beneath unrelenting floods. To avoid this fate, say the environmentalists, we must accept extensive changes to the economy, and to the way we live our lives.

There is no debate to be had about this, urge the climate alarmists. It is as if the real policymakers arrive at Westminster, Brussels and Strasburg and at the UN on horseback. War, Famine, Plague and Pestilence themselves seem to have issued the directives instructing us how much water our washing machines may use and how powerful our vacuum cleaners may be, and which light bulbs we may use to light our homes (Directive 2009/125/EC). At the other end of The Grid, directives from Europe dictate how much of which fuels may be used to generate electricity, and when (Directives 2010/75/EU, 2001/80/EC, 2009/28/EC, and many more).

For those who hold with classical-liberal thinking this is worrying in many respects. The threat of extreme weather has been used to justify central planning. And it has put central planning out of the reach of rational democratic processes, under the control of technocrats. Climate and energy policies are argued for on the basis of scientific authority, but are driven by mythology – a green theocracy's Book of Revelation.

Extreme weather

We are now used to stories of extreme weather ... The hottest year ever... The wettest summer... The mildest January... The driest March... For a decade... Century... Since records began. The garden thermometer barely has to register a sunny day before someone will link it to climate change. A series of mild winters prompts articles about how children 'won't know what snow is'. When the snows return to these shores with vengeance, the same newspapers glibly announce, 'this is what global warming looks like'. Rivers have burst their banks since men first started engineering the land. But the first signs of floods brings out climate change alarmism as sure as spring brings out the daffodils.

Early 2014 brought some Southern parts of Britain the wettest weather they had ever seen. This was, for sure, 'extreme weather'. Throughout January and February, TV news and the front pages of newspapers were dominated by dramatic images of disruption to transport, and waves smashing into crumbling coastlines. Floods and storms like these were going to be the 'new normal', claimed the climate pundits, many of whom had said the same thing about the winter and spring drought that England experienced just two years earlier. The Met Office dutifully announced that the drought was set to continue through the summer. But rather than being remembered as the year of the 'worst prediction ever made', 2012 is remembered for having the 'wettest summer for 100 years'. The summer was the same as it was a century ago... because of climate change. The summer of 2012 was even wetter than the 'Barbecue Summer', the Met Office had predicted just three years earlier. Climatologists are the slowest people to learn from the weather.

If you only watched the news in early 2014, you could be forgiven for believing that the entire country had been submerged. But of Britain's 25 million homes, fewer than 6,000 were flooded. That is cold, wet comfort for the occupants of those homes, of course. But it is put in perspective by the floods of 2007, when 48,461 homes were flooded, 23,000 of them in my constituency, Yorkshire. Extreme rainfall and an extremely wet winter it may have been, but the flooding was not, by any historical measure of Britain's floods, extreme.

The 1928 Thames flood inundated Central London, including the House of Commons. It claimed 14 lives and 4,000 homes. In Lynmouth in 1953, 34 people were killed and over 400 made homeless, a tragedy I remember from my youth only too well. The same year, the North Sea flood killed a further 326 Britons on the East Coast of England and Scotland. Nearly 400 square miles were submerged. Tens of thousands were evacuated. In 1968, floods throughout the summer and autumn were far worse for the Home Counties and Somerset than the floods of early 2014. More than

12,000 homes were affected in Surrey alone. But even the mid-twentieth Century floods look like mere paddling pools when compared to the Great Storm of 1703, which took as many as 15,000 lives.

It is a remarkable thing that flooding claims so few lives and so few properties today, compared to yesteryear. But nobody is blaming climate change for our improved protection from the elements. Given the political will and the cash resources, the infrastructure and planning necessary to protect people and property was put in place within a generation or two. Now, fatalities caused by flooding are a rare thing indeed. The risks to properties have been massively reduced. Britain is safer from the elements than it has ever been. But environmentalists will tell you that the winter of 2013-4 was the worst since Noah. This calls for an explanation.

Our understanding of risks is entirely skewed. We are taught what to be afraid of. Politicians and environmental activists love to remind us that climate change is the 'biggest problem facing mankind'. But is it really the biggest threat to your home and to your family's security?

Between 2004 and 2009, the number of homes repossessed rose from 8,500 a year to 48,900 out of around 11.3 million mortgaged properties. Since then, there have been around 35,000 a year. Over the course of 9 years, more than a quarter of a million homes were taken away. Not by the seas or rivers, but by banks and the courts. That's 1% of all homes in less than a decade – a real manmade disaster. If we are concerned about our homes, the numbers show us that we are exposed to much greater risks from the mismanaged economy than we are from the weather. Yet the climate dominates the political agenda and the news. Why?

The scale of this distraction is phenomenal. Imagine for a moment that floods in Britain swept away one per cent of homes each decade. It really would be impossible to resist the outrage. TV news teams rush to film end-of-the-world sequences the moment it looks like a river may reach a few inches beneath some unfortunate person's home. But they take almost no interest in the tens of thousands of people evicted from their homes each year. No outside broadcasts for them. Climate change – previously known as weather – is a much more interesting spectacle.

This is not the chapter for a full discussion about what 'extreme weather' is a distraction from. Suffice it to say that the public discussion of risk is skewed, and that this misconception benefits the mismanagers and over-managers of public life. Politicians are a bigger threat to your home than the contents of clouds will ever be. There is less loss of life and damage to property today than there was in the past. Yet the political establishment, the media and many academics will tell you that the risks of 'extreme weather' are growing.

But perhaps you are not yet convinced. Then let us look more closely at this idea of 'extreme weather'. What is it? To you and me, 'extreme weather' sounds like weather that is destructive in its own right. But there is a problem with this understanding – what is 'extreme' for one place is not extreme for another.

The average temperature in Singapore is 27°C. In London, the average temperature in summer is just 16°C. In winter, it is just 4.5°C. The coldest place on the planet in the heart of Antarctica reaches minus 93°C. In Death Valley in California, the temperature has been recorded as high as 56.7°C. The difference between these two extremes is nearly 150°C. The wettest places on the planet experience more than 472" of rain per year. London has just 29.5". What is average weather in one place may be completely benign in another. What is mild weather in one place is extreme elsewhere.

'Extreme' weather is not extreme by virtue of the phenomenon itself, but by where and when it occurs. A typical British summer would be an 'extreme' thing in the Arctic – mild is extreme at the extremes. Extreme weather is weather that is statistically unusual in one place. It means nothing else. Extreme weather is not, on this definition, especially violent weather. Mild weather can be 'extreme' weather. Environmentalists have exploited the difference between the everyday and scientific understandings of the word 'extreme' – although many scientists have been complicit in the deception – to further their agenda. Bad weather is not allowed to be simply bad weather anymore, because weather has become political.

Campaigners for action on climate change have been promising us that weather which is now extreme (i.e. rare for the place it occurs), will become more frequent. And they have said that storms and floods have become more common. This was science, they claimed. Unfortunately for the environmentalists, however, when the scientists came to audit the world's weather, they found otherwise. The Intergovernmental Panel on Climate Change (IPCC) is amongst the organisations which made such forecasts in the past. But their 2012 review of the scientific evidence of changing weather extremes, Managing the Risks of Extreme Events and Disasters to Advance Climate Change Adaptation (SREX), found little to be afraid of.

IPCC SREX found that "There is medium evidence and high agreement that long-term trends in normalised losses have not been attributed to natural or anthropogenic climate change". In other words, scientists have been unable to establish that climate change had caused a single penny's worth of damage. It continued, "the statement about the absence of trends in impacts attributable to natural or anthropogenic climate change holds for tropical and extratropical storms and tornados". We have long been promised more frequent and intense storms, but the science said that they had not yet arrived, and that no economic effect from them was detectable. And it got worse for the alarmists. "The absence of an attributable climate change signal in losses also holds for flood losses".

The IPCC did claim, however, that it had "medium confidence" that it had "more likely than not" detected an "increase in the frequency, intensity, and/or amount of heavy precipitation", and that it had "very likely" detected warmer days and nights throughout the world. But the link between catastrophic weather extremes and manmade climate change was now broken. The world was no more vulnerable to floods, droughts, storms and wildfires than it was half a century ago.

Even the increased frequency or intensity of rain, linked to climate change by the IPCC, has not produced an increase in flooding. The IPCC even admits it cannot rule out the possibility that there are fewer floods today, than in the past. This is what global warming looks like. Extreme weather might mean nothing more than a few more warm days in autumn, an inch more rain in April, fewer frosty winter mornings, and a few more summer heat waves a decade. The climate Apocalypse looks almost pleasant.

The extent to which these changes in our climate – if they are occurring at all – will cause problems is determined by our ability to cope with them. The bigger difference to the outcome of extreme weather is made, not by the weather itself, but our flood and coastal defences, the capacity of our rivers and other flood defences, and the resilience of our transport network. The media love to point out that "the wettest winter for fifty years" causes problems. But problems that were surmountable 50 years ago are surely more easily overcome today. If floods are more frequent today, it is not because it rains more. It is because our planners and policymakers have the wrong priorities. That was the terrible lesson of Hurricane Katrina. It wasn't the storm that caused New Orleans to be inundated by the storm surge; it was the failure to maintain the levees that protected it.

It must be noted now, that as well as there being no significant change detected in extreme weather events at the global level, there has been no rise in the temperature of the planet for nearly 20 years. This should force a long hard look at the claims made by climate activists, British, EU and UK politicians and journalists over the last three decades or more.

Extreme politics

Environmentalism is an extreme political ideology. By 'environmentalism' I do not mean simply the scruffy looking 'chuggers' from green organisations, who raise money on the High Street for illegal activities on the high seas and other places. I mean also the greens of the Great and the Good, the media, the establishment, and politicians from the old parties, in Westminster and in Brussels. The story of extreme weather has been pushed by them, for their own advantage, against the public's interest. It is no coincidence, for example, that those who are most committed to handing British sovereignty to Europe are the most inclined to climate change alarmism. European federalists need myths like extreme weather and climate change.

One clue that environmentalism is an extreme ideology is that in the debate about extreme weather, there has rarely been any middle ground offered by environmentalists. Climate change was never going to make the weather slightly different, and perhaps a bit worse than normal, sometimes. An environmentalist's rage is as visceral as the mad Ayatollah's. Both are uncompromising. It is their way, or fire and brimstone. A failure to do what the environmentalist says means nothing less than total catastrophe. An environmentalist can only speak about extreme weather, because to talk about merely slightly different or slightly worse weather would be to admit that other principles or values might inform debate.

Another clue that environmentalism is extreme is to understand what the environmentalists' vision is. As far as I am able to tell, environmentalists desire most to control the production and consumption of material resources. For some this means abandoning economic growth and technological progress, and even wealth itself. Others are perhaps more reluctant to attach themselves to such radical ideas. Yet they seek control nonetheless. Their reluctance is perhaps owed to the fact that environmentalism is not, and never has been, a vote-winner.

The recognition that environmentalism is unpopular is our third and biggest clue about its extreme, totalitarian nature. The disgraced former Secretary of State for Climate Change and Energy, Chris Huhne once told the BBC that

"All through human political history, you have had governments that have tried to set up particular objectives and have realised they can only go so far so fast without the rest of the world going along with them. For example, back in the bad old days of communism, you had the whole argument about whether Joe Stalin could have socialism in one country. You can't have environmentalism in one country."

Candid words from Huhne. Indeed, you can't have environmentalism in one country... because nobody would vote for it, given a choice. The problem of choice was therefore overcome by taking choice away from the public. Environmentalism won few votes at ballot boxes, but a green theocracy dominates the EU and UN nonetheless. Nobody in Europe has had the opportunity to vote for or against the directives that the EC has issued about carbon emissions, renewable energy or light bulbs. Together, these policies will have caused European billpayers direct costs of trillions of Euros. The indirect costs are incalculable. These costs were incurred to prevent extreme weather, which the IPCC have agreed is not detectable. And even if it were, there is even less evidence that the EU's policies would have done anything to stop extreme weather.

Climate, energy and environmental policies are increasingly the subject of central planning, rather than either democratic or market control. The UN has, since 1990, attempted to establish a global agreement that will limit each country's carbon emissions. The EU has gone further, hoping to lead this process, by also requiring member states to produce certain amounts of so-called 'renewable energy', and by creating Emissions-Trading schemes, amongst many other interventions. The current UK government and its opposition want to lead even this process, and so quangos and technocrats have established an even stricter regime, unopposed by supine MPs, which will suck the life out of the British economy by sending energy prices skywards.

Eisenhower, a great General, a plausible President and unbelievably prescient thinker foresaw in his farewell speech many of the problems we face today. He warned that research, the province of universities until the 1950s, driven by intellectual curiosity and the rules of scientific discipline would be replaced by scientists in the pay of federal government as budgets balloon as indeed they have done. This inevitably results in 'political' science.

If someone's salary, and therefore mortgage and educational fees, depends on a government grant, it is probable that someone will not rock the boat. I simply discount scientific 'evidence' produced by anyone paid by a special interest group. Government in particular. Sadly, now this even includes the Royal Society, heavily subsidised by the exchequer.

I publish in full here Mark Twain's amusing piece from Life on the Mississippi. He foresaw the lazy and unimaginative scientist of today based on those of his time. Imagine the nonsense if the computer model had it been a scientific toy then. What Prince of Wales or President of the Royal Society would not have bought into the prediction that the Mississippi would be one and three quarter miles long and how that would end the world as we know it?

I listened to our current Prince of Wales address us in the European Parliament last year buying into the computer model scam lock, stock and barrel. Before we filed in, it was made absolutely clear we could neither heckle nor question. One wonders who sits in his Royal Highness's outer office censoring anything that might resemble common sense. No wonder his father is reported to despair of him.

Once there was a neck opposite Port Hudson, Louisiana, which was only half a mile across, in its narrowest place. You could walk across there in fifteen minutes; but if you made the journey around the cape on a raft, you travelled thirty five miles to accomplish the same thing. In 1722 the river darted through that neck, deserted its old bed, and thus shortened itself thirty five miles. In the same way it shortened itself twenty five miles at Black Hawk Point in 1699. Below Red River Landing, Raccourci cut off was made (forty or fifty years ago I think). This shortened the river twenty eight miles. In our day, if you travel by river from the southernmost of these three cut-offs to the northernmost, you go only seventy miles. To do the same thing a hundred and seventy six years ago, one had to go a hundred and fifty eight miles! A shortening of eighty eight miles in that trifling distance. At some forgotten time in the past, cut-offs were made above Vidalia, Louisiana; at island 92, at island 84 and at Hale's Point. These shortened the river, in the aggregate, seventy seven miles.

Since my own day on the Mississippi, cut-offs have been made at Hurricane Island; at island 100; at

Napoleon, Arkansas, at Walnut Bend, and at Council Bend. These shortened the river, in the aggregate, sixty seven miles. In my own time a cut off was made at American Bend, which shortened the river ten miles or more.

"Therefore, the Mississippi between Cairo and New Orleans was twelve hundred and fifteen miles long one hundred and seventy six years ago. It was eleven hundred and eighty after the cut-off of 1722. It was one thousand and forty after the American Bend cut-off. It has lost sixty seven miles since. Consequently its length is only nine hundred and seventy three miles at present.

Now, if I wanted to be one of those ponderous scientific people and 'let on' to prove what had occurred in a given time in the recent past, or what will occur in the far future by what has occurred in late years, what an opportunity is here! Geology never had such a chance, nor such exact data to argue from! Nor 'development of species', either! Glacial epochs are great things, but they are vague-vague.

Please observe: in the space of one hundred and seventy six years the Lower Mississippi has shortened itself two hundred and forty two miles. That is an average of a trifle over one mile and a third per year. Therefore, any calm person, who is not blind, idiotic, can see that in the Old Oölitic Silurian Period, just a million years ago next November, the Lower Mississippi River was upwards of one million, three hundred thousand miles long, and stuck out over the Gulf of Mexico like a fishing-rod. And by the same token any person can see that seven hundred and forty two years from now the Lower Mississippi will be only a mile and three quarters long, and Cairo and New Orleans will have joined their streets together and be plodding comfortably along under a single mayor and mutual board of aldermen. There is something fascinating about science. One gets such wholesale returns of conjecture out of such a trifling investment of fact.

Chapter 5
Driving

There are 33 million drivers in the UK. It is therefore highly unlikely if you are reading this book you are not a driver. For the last twenty years you have been made to feel guilty about being one. The drip, drip, drip government propagate that somehow, because you drive, you are a bad citizen. This is of course absurd but the reason it is done is anything but. It is quite deliberately to make you cowed. When you are cowed, defeated, guilty you are ready to be fleeced. Last year I was driving along a major A road in Yorkshire, central reservation dual carriageway for sixty miles, the road is derestricted. There is a completely anomalous stretch of about 800 yards which is restricted to 40 mph. A mobile camera trawls people in every day. It is a scam. Obviously a scam. So downtrodden is the motorist, so unorganised and unrepresented, they just pay up. The fundamental principles of English law have been suspended in order to fleece the motorist. His road tax goes nowhere near roads, the VAT at 20% on his car is extortionate, over three quarters of the price of a tank of diesel or petrol goes straight to the government, much of which bails out incompetent bankers.

In a sleepy, empty Durham market town just a few weeks ago on a Sunday morning I parked quite safely in a bay outside my hotel to load our luggage. It was a loading bay, restricted apparently to people loading who were not us. £35. There is no time or system for a citizen to object, weeks of correspondence and eventually a £75 fine. I paid. This is theft. Had it been a mugger I would have called the police. It was the council. As always it is the state, not the mugger, you need fear; everyone is regularly robbed by the state, very few by a criminal.

Would you believe that with countless road safety charities, foundations, lobby groups, parliamentary advisors and partnerships, after some three hundred billion driver miles a year, there are fewer deaths on UK's roads from any cause than from accidents in the home and five times less than from NHS failure? You could ask why, if death and injury were the real concern, are we not focussing more on the NHS or in people's kitchens too.

Well, maybe the answer could be that behind all of the seemingly laudable schemes and proposals, there is money to be made.

Why are we so unaware of it? Why are UK's largest voting block, its drivers, so resigned and compliant to so much exploitation, prosecution and official hostility against them?

Perhaps this is an answer. CURACAO, (Coordination of urban road-user charging organisational issues) advises councils to use various tricks to push through road pricing schemes, including: Promising low charges then rapidly increasing them once the scheme is in place. - False 'trial periods' to make people think the scheme will be re-evaluated when there is no such intention. - Avoiding referenda at all costs. - Using a psychological trick called 'Dissonance Theory' to make people believe that road pricing or policy is inevitable and that 'resistance is futile'. This also induces effects like less anger, less resistance,

weaker intentions to protect their freedoms. In other words, their minds should be manipulated.' Keith Peat, Drivers' Union November 2008.

Although the foregoing was about road pricing schemes, there is evidence that use of cognitive dissonance in government is being applied to many situations; never more so than road safety policy.

We are persuaded by motor car salesmen that we enjoy driving. This is very important because governments tax people who are enjoying themselves. How many argue with the mantra 'driving is a privilege'? It is not. It is no more a privilege than cooking, washing, ironing and going to work. Most of us see it as a chore with massive liability, cost and worry. We do it because we need to. Our society and economy is based on car ownership and drivers. Is 'driving is a privilege' the primary mind bender for drivers?

Nearly all of the alleged road safety registered charities, foundations and advisory bodies have agendas other than road safety and are often green anti-driver lobby groups, whose CEOs are very well remunerated with cash and very often honours. It is rare to find a genuine road safety charity that combines expertise with true altruism without other agendas.

Such a lack of expertise in air safety would be a national scandal.

How can thirty five million drivers, a massive voting block, be completely discounted, oppressed, taxed, prosecuted, jailed, exploited and fleeced so easily if it were not by applying cognitive dissonance?

The language the industry uses is deliberately disarming and benign. 'Speed kills!' 'Calming'. 'Living streets' 'It is 30 for a reason' 'Shared space'. 'One person dies on the road every 30 seconds' 'Safety camera'. Yet it all has one objective. To remove private cars from the road and to promote public transport. Attempt to challenge the rhetoric and experience the aggression accompanied by an avalanche of bogus statistics.

One charity, in the usual emotive manner, tells us 'One person dies on the road every 30 seconds' How can anyone not be moved by it? Except that people are not dying every 30 seconds in the UK, where the charities are based, but in third world countries, where it is happening and where road safety is way at the bottom of their priority list. Malnutrition, disease, despotism, war, and corruption tops their priority list. In the UK, the death rate is far lower at about every 16000 seconds. How strange then that the charities are based here, where the money is, instead of in third world countries where they are needed most.

None of this benign rhetoric stands close examination.

The setting of speed limits is now totally arbitrary. 'It is 30 for a reason.' is quite false too because valid reasons are rarely advanced to apply a speed limit.

How many challenge 'Speed kills!' the very goldmine of sound bites? It is false. Speed is motion and motion is speed. I travelled home from Brazil recently in a Boeing 777 at 550 mph and lived to tell the tale.

Why should any honest proposition need to use dishonest or disguised rhetoric in road safety? Road safety and prosecutions are far too serious to be the subject of spin and sound bite. Why do we accept 'safety camera' when a speed camera cannot detect safety and is only to measure speed?

We only have to look at the speeding industry where drivers are actually encouraged to increase speed by road layout so that limited companies may profit from dishonest driver courses. When we hear of a camera site that generates thousands of offenders why is that allowed to continue? If they were accidents should police just take pictures or find out what is going wrong?

To facilitate this, officials turn yet again to spin. 'Excessive speed' is not even in the Road Traffic Act so why use terms that are not recognised in the law unless of course with the deliberate intent to confuse 'speeding' which cannot cause anything, with too fast, an element of dangerous driving, that does? The problem for the speeding industry is that, because too fast is often below the limits and speed cameras cannot detect it as well as drunk, drugged, dangerous, careless, distracted, texting or sleepy drivers, it means that the instrument of generating so much money for them, cannot detect one single accident cause at all. Not in the speed awareness syllabus.

It is very similar to a yellow box junction where one has already generated £2.7 million for its council in one year. Clearly the yellow box is not working but the council are not interested in that but in revenue. Just as another council gathering £6.8 million from its bus lanes between April 12 and February 14. All this is usually caused by road layout or poor or confusing signage that can easily be corrected. When one unitary area revealed that their budget was based on 18000 speeders a year, and another area are selling an average of 6000 speed awareness courses a month, what incentive is there to actually prevent the offending and addressing the problem when there is so much revenue generation?

Why do we all fall for the pious indignation of profiteers when challenged? Billions of pounds taken from our economy every year and none of these costly items stop one single accident.

What we currently have is a policy of corrupt, profit-based, prosecution of many thousands of perfectly safe drivers. Dishonest speed and driver awareness courses run by private firms. We now have coercive deals to accept guilt on payment of money to a limited company when it was once accepted that police officers who took money in lieu of a judicial process went to gaol? How have we come to this?

The problem with the road safety industry is insatiable. It must feed itself. When one unitary authority concedes that high volumes of speeding offenders is part of their budget, then we can see that part of the process is to keep lowering the bar on drivers. More reasons to fail an MOT, lowering the drink drive limit, lowering speed limits, all keep the test, camera and instrument manufacturers and course providers and sign writers in business.

Road safety policy has been developed piecemeal for over a hundred years. The current Highway Code is a microcosm of such flawed road safety. It has grown to a 145 page tome of 307 rules as well as 15 pages of road signs, markings and signals- the original had only 15 signs- all to be learned by rote to pass a test and just as easily forgotten. Are drivers really expected to mentally recall all these rules whilst crashing or making driving decisions? Much of it is out of date and irrelevant to the 21st Century.

Chapter 6

Law

According to the Daily Telegraph I was the first man since John Wilkes to be booted out of the Mansion House for heckling the Gilbertian figure of Lord Turner, quangocrat extraordinaire. Legitimate therefore perhaps I quote William Pitt in his speech on the Wilkes case of January 1770. 'Where laws end, tyranny begins'.

As a politician, at least for the time being, I am often struck by the number of people who come up after a lecture or speech to suggest politics should be taught in schools. They mean of course, party politics, already dismissed as worthless in another chapter. What they mean are the principles of law. This should be a compulsory subject at middle school age. As English law is a birthright it is vital young people are aware of it, as politicians steal it piecemeal on an almost daily basis.

The first question to address is what is the law for? Without law, particularly property protection, there can be no foundation for the state. The law is to protect everyone and no-one is exempted from it. The law is the bastion that protects the citizen or subject from politicians, Kings, despots and gangsters. Without it the state is doomed to failure. It is worth noting countries and continents rich in natural resources still founder. Argentina has been an emerging market since the late 19th Century. Much of Africa is a basket case, Russia takes one pace forward and two back every few years. Without property rights there can be no entrepreneurship, no foreign investment and no growth in living standards. Political systems are of less importance than the rule of law. Let us look at English Law, which has been at the root of the economic success of the Anglosphere in the last two hundred years. What are the fundamental principles? Why is it so admired and often copied?

Traditional common law presumes the innocence of the accused. The development of this principle is over one thousand years old; it extends further back than Magna Carta to the time of King Alfred.

The next principle is habeas corpus which came much later. Any charge must be backed by prima facie evidence. A British subject must be charged within twenty four hours of arrest, with special permission from a Magistrate to extend to ninety six hours.

The third pillar is trial by jury. A concept of justice first enshrined in Magna Carta, albeit only extended to those of noble birth. There are other rights for the subject - double jeopardy; you can only be tried once for an offence. There is a right to silence, the inadmissibility of hearsay evidence, previous convictions are withheld from the court. There are others but this is not a primer for law students but an aide memoire for those who are currently enjoying the protection of a system once the envy of the world.

Why is common law such a good thing? No man, or group of men or women, could possibly draw up a book of law to meet every conceivable circumstance. It matters not how many brilliant minds were assembled. Common law is formed by judicial precedence, in other words that which has gone before. This gives access for the court to hundreds of years of wisdom and judgements. This fantastic reservoir is available to us all. It supports statute law formed by parliament, amended where necessary by the House of Lords before receiving Royal Assent.

Another invaluable time-honoured protection is that no parliament may bind a subsequent parliament. In short, bad law can be rescinded. I had the great honour to meet a Supreme Court judge in Washington two years ago, incidentally where they have an original fair copy of Magna Carta upon which system their law is based. He made a very impressive point which stayed with me, "laws should be difficult to make". His point being to impose law on fellow citizens should not be undertaken lightly.

So, we in the United Kingdom should be safe from tyranny, should we not? Our age-old system is at work still. Well, no, I fear it is being eroded gradually but surely to an extent impossible for me to have conceived when I was sweating through some law exams in the 1960s.

Let me outline the many ways politicians steal this birthright like a thief in the night.

What could possibly go wrong? A system of law deeply set in concrete, matured over nine hundred years which has withstood assault by Europe's greatest despots? The Royal Navy and more latterly the Royal Air Force have kept our island race secure to work and play under the protection of the law within a constitutional monarchy. A system of legal government for which millions have given their lives in combat to secure. No amount of force could wrest this birthright from us. So why is it seeping away? What evil force is destabilising the nation and how are they doing it?

The enemy within first take away the knowledge of that birthright. They play the long game. They control the curriculum through a state school system to which even the private system must comply to furnish students with their absurd pieces of paper without which it is impossible even to be called for an interview for the most mundane of white-collar jobs.

The relentless assault on the principles of English Law continue through the British Institutions. The drip, drip of undermining confidence in the English law is promulgated by the bland grey spokesmen representing the Chatham House Fifth Column. I heard one say at an institutional lecture a few years ago that common law was 'archaic and cumbersome' and was better replaced with Corpus Juris or Napoleonic Code prescriptive legislation. Sad little man with his pseudo tidy little mind with a second-class honours degree from Oxford condemning nine hundred years of history sporting his cheap suit and polyester tie. I desperately wanted to kick his arse.

We have moved to a system where our laws are now made by an unelected bureaucratic European

Commissioner with a European 'Parliament' the amending chamber. What an extraordinary abrogation of responsibility for our elected representatives, quite illegal under the British Constitution and contrary even to Her Majesty's Coronation oath.

One is immediately reminded of John of Gaunt's speech from Shakespeare's Richard II "With inky blots, and rotten parchment bonds, that England, that was wont to conquer others has made a shameful conquest of itself".

Habeus Corpus, that pillar of English law ceases to apply to the European Arrest Warrant as has the need for prima facie evidence, trial by jury and the presumption of innocence. Policemen from any one of twenty seven European countries can spirit an Englishman away with none of their protections for supposed offences which do not exist in English law. Indeed, they have done so; they are well documented. How can the nation have been failed by every line of defence, the Commons, Lords, free press, public service broadcasting even Her Majesty? Every day there is another effort to remove these pillars and not just by subservience to Brussels. Trial by jury is under constant threat. It is administratively inconvenient. Would it not be easier to rush people through a veneer of judicial system to save expense? I have heard supposedly educated men suggest that trial by jury should be unavailable for theft of small amounts. How could it matter to an honest citizen if he were wrongly convicted of theft for £10 or £1,000?

How else do they steal this birthright? Behold the Enabling Acts. A law comes from an unelected body, the European Commission, or Westminster. The enforcement is made by a British Quango. An amazing example was the Financial Services Authority. They were granted super powers by an enabling act, produced a prescriptive rule book of over 4 million words, interpreted them subjectively, adjudicated on them, apportioned fines, pocketed the money and no court of appeal. Every single principle of English Law abandoned. Only a judicial review available and that made financially prohibitive. Incidentally, press coverage is illegal except the release by the authority post investigation. It might be worth looking up the salaries and pensions of the employees. You will not find their experience in financial services published, it is a secret.

For the motorist, one of 33 million citizens in the UK, I have devoted another chapter. The complete abandonment of law has led to mass state theft from the biggest unrepresented group in Europe.

The Abuse of Law

It is not enough to have a worthy legal system. The United Kingdom should be the benchmark for any constitutional democracy. The legal system has developed over a thousand years and therefore can claim to have been tested and retested by circumstances beyond imagination. Total war, civil war, pestilence, huge political changes. Until relatively recently the system remained stretched but unbroken. The United States adopted the English legal system almost in its entirety but decided upon a written constitution, the obvious goal to enshrine the system and protect it against the inevitable corruption endemic to mankind and especially the political class. Sadly, the invasion of the free trade southern states by the industrialised protectionist northern states meant that the subsequent United States became centralised administratively - a disadvantage from which the country has never recovered.

In my view, the Constitution has been all but abandoned, the Supreme Court, now like Britain has its highest judges appointed by journeymen politicians to the detriment of the same principles. The state system? Plea bargaining. Bang up the accused in conditions unworthy of a medieval dungeon, postpone trial until the victim is prepared to confess to anything. Shamefully the UK signed up to a treaty to send British citizens into this system without prima facie evidence. The Christopher Tippins case is an example. I would imprison Jack Straw and Bob Ainsworth for putting through the US Treaty and the European Arrest Warrant until they made a televised apology in a hair shirt.

Two major world wars broke the British system welding a national suffrage system joined at the hip to welfarism. Everyday access therefore to the law of the land and those principles was curtailed and the low-level magistrates' courts changed from being the first line of defence for the citizen to become a stick with which to beat him. The presumption of innocence is almost completely ignored at this level as a minor offender will confirm. Justice under the law becomes the preserve of the wealthy. I have friends who have accepted a caution, although completely innocent, to save time and money wasted in the Magistrates' kangaroo system. The latest manifestation of this is the householder defending his property or family; there are too many examples of this for me to need to elaborate here.

Historically there have been a number of government administrative systems. Capitalism, communism, socialism, fascism and mercantilism, there are subdivisions and various mixtures. Communism was based on the ownership of production, fascism the control of production. The constitutional democracies have sleep walked into fascism. They control by regulation. There is now almost no aspect of production not regulated. It therefore is outside the law and its founding principles. This manifests itself in extraordinary ways, always to the detriment of small businesses, which are the pillars of a free economy across the world. Perhaps one of the most horrifying in recent years was the west country dairy herd, slaughtered because the paperwork was faulty. The High Court Judge accepted the herd was healthy but seemed denied the role of administering natural justice to the farmer involved. Again, there are too many of such cases to list here.

I have been closely involved with regulation in the financial service sector. I have had experience of compliance and, at second hand, enforcement. Under English law there is no compromise; the law is the law, it is interpreted by Judges and put before a jury. It is argued in open court by those trained in the law. Regulation is no such thing. It is loosely worded by those often without experience of financial services. The whole approach to interpretation is subjective. I remember going to a consultation briefing on regulation and playing buzz word bingo. Here are a few. Safety, soundness, robust, unfair, deceptive and abusive, excessive, client's best interests, transparent, risk awareness. There are, of course, many more. This nonsense pervades most of the Anglosphere. Meaningless jargon. I suspect that the other regulatory authorities have the same self-serving oligarchical approach. Regulation is an industry. Big businesses are not so adversely affected. Big salaries for compliance staff and consultancy back up are not a problem especially as it is loaded onto the customer. There is no hiding place for small businesses, moreover they can be closed down on a whim. He is by definition not too big to fail.

Most middle Englanders now have no access to their birthright on a day to day basis. His protection has been removed and he is at the mercy of the regulator or his Jack-in-office enforcer. Farming, finance and retail all suffer the tyranny of the sort of individual portrayed in Dad's Army, the warden Hodges. Western democracies need a bonfire of quangos and regulation and return to law.

Chapter 7

The 39 Articles

I felt it might be worthwhile to have a look at another state institution which has been mute as our system of government moves overseas. In England for better or worse we have state religion with the monarch at its head. It is not nearly as supine as most people believe. UKIP regularly achieves two to three million votes in various elections, it has three peers in the upper chamber. The Anglican church has more. Apart from the knee-jerk reaction to welfare reform they are deeply embedded in the establishment and all too often in matters of constitutional importance they can be relied upon to behave as noddy dogs. How did it all start?

In the year 668 a monk named Theodore, aged 66, was quietly getting on with his life of prayer and study in the Cilesian Monastery in Rome when Pope Vitalian singled him out to be appointed Archbishop of Canterbury. He was to be the last Antiochian Orthodox Archbishop of Canterbury.

Theodore was born in Tarsus, not far from Antioch. When he was about 10 years old, he went to study at the famous schools in Antioch. It was the nearest thing to what we would call a university education today. Over the next few years he continued his studies both there and in Edessa, Syria. These covered medicine, mathematics, astronomy - where he specialised in being able to work out the date of Easter correctly - philosophy, public speaking, and of course Biblical studies.

In his mid-thirties Arab raiders overran Tarsus and Antioch, and we find Theodore studying and teaching in Constantinople. About ten years later he moved to Rome.

Following his consecration, he made his way to England and it was here that his years of study came to fruition. What he found when he got here was a chaotic church. Bishops were even unsure of the geographical boundaries of their dioceses. So at the age of sixty seven, a remarkable age in those times, he set off throughout the country and fixed the boundaries of the dioceses. These boundaries remain more or less intact until this day, with a few more dioceses carved out of them, to account, for example, for the mobility of labour in the Industrial Revolution. Mind you, if you crossed Theodore he could divide a diocese himself, as he did when he deposed Wilfred of York, and divided the diocese of Northumbria into three, with new bishops.

Having sorted out the diocesan boundaries, he then decided to help things on with a book of rules, the Ten Canons, to be observed by the entire Church of England. This must have come as a surprise to the previously disorganised clergy, but it seems to have worked, and as the church touched everyone in the land he has been referred to as the Father of England. His Canons remain more or less intact today.

Politically he was a persuasive and successful man. Around the time of the Council of Hatfield, near Doncaster, in the heart of my constituency which he called to condemn Monothelitism a year before it was condemned by the Sixth Œcumenical Council, he consecrated a local Lincolnshire monk, Æthelwine, bishop to hold the fort while he set off to reconcile the warring kings of Northumbria and Mercia.

How unlike the milksop Archbishops of Canterbury of recent years.

Now this reorganised Church of England still had a foreign bishop as it ultimate head - the Bishop of Rome. This was probably in the minds of the authors of the Magna Carta, where the very first Article reads 'the English Church shall be free'. It needed to be free of the situation where vast tracts of land and property belonged to the dioceses that Theodore had set up so many centuries earlier, and to the monasteries that had flourished following the Norman invasion. The church was answerable to the Bishop of Rome, not to the crown, and this rankled.

It was in the reign of Richard II that a serious attempt was made to put a stop to money leaving for Rome, for appeals being made to Rome, and so on. In the Statute of Præmunire we read that if any purchase or pursue, or cause to be purchased or pursued in the court of Rome or elsewhere, any such translations, processes, and sentences of excommunications, bulls, instruments or any other things whatsoever .. he and his notaries, abettors, and counsellors shall be put out of the king's protection and their lands escheat - which usually meant that they reverted to the crown.

Henry VIII too dug in his heels about the same matter in the Act in Restraint of Appeals to Rome, written by Thomas Cromwell, where reference is made to the 'dangers, pains, and penalties contained and limited in the Act of Provision and Præmunire made in the sixteenth year of the king's most noble progenitor King Richard II'.

This supremacy of the English throne was of course a problem when the UK government planned to enter a European Union, so these laws were repealed in the Criminal Justice Act of 1967. However, the Church of England's own book of rules, the 39 Articles of Religion is clear about the legal status of rule from beyond the national boundaries. In Article 37 we read 'The King's Majesty hath the chief power in this Realm of England and other his Dominions unto whom the chief Government of all Estates of this Realm, whether they be Ecclesiastical or Civil, in all causes doth appertain, and is not, nor ought to be, subject to any foreign Jurisdiction.' Today all clergy beneficed in the Church of England, assent to these Thirty Nine Articles, all thirty nine!

You can find the 39 Articles in the Book of Common Prayer, but they have been omitted from current dumbed-down official prayer books. Younger generations will not be able to browse through their modern prayer book and read them during long-winded sermons about climate change, or whatever is the latest topic that will avoid the need to mention that Christ is God and is to be worshipped. Gone too in the new books are the State Prayers. Henry VIII knew how to deal with such backsliders.

So what about the Archbishops, are they now free to support handing over the government of this country to a foreign power? After all, the Archbishop of Canterbury is still next in precedence to the Queen's cousins, so should be on-side, and the Archbishop of York is above the Prime Minister on the precedence list. Both Archbishops are Privy Counsellors by right, but still have to take the Privy Counsellor's oath. It reads 'You will to your uttermost bear Faith and Allegiance to the Queen's Majesty; and will assist and defend all civil and temporal Jurisdictions, Pre-eminences, and Authorities, granted to Her Majesty and annexed by Acts of Parliament, or otherwise, against all Foreign Princes, Persons, Prelates, States, or Potentates.' Have you ever heard the Paxmans or Humphries of this world put this to a churchman?

You will have to search hard to find a bishop who is a Eurorealist and not Europhile. After all, as the appointments are in the hands of the Prime Minister, and as the Prime Minister at the time of the appointment tolerates England's membership - which all have done - then it is a done deal; the Church of England is bound up with the 'European Project'. The Synod of 1972 commended the Church of England 'to take full advantage of Britain's membership of the European Economic Community'. The General Synod's Board of Social Responsibility in 1995 positively eulogised the

European Project. Today we have a recommendation to voters in the European Elections to vote for a stronger EU as 'the current situation - (whatever they mean by that) - endangers the goals of the European Project'. Fortunately, no one takes notice of the Anglican church today electorally.

In the last century there were between 105 and 110 active bishops in the Church of England at any one time, but it looks as though they are cutting back. As I write, a dozen or so seats are vacant. how many will be filled again is something we wait to see. Bishops are a bit expensive, and although giving by members of the C of E is generous, it cannot be expected to cover a burgeoning bureaucracy both at episcopal and Synodical level. Already when the Bishop of the Cathedral See of Ripon and Leeds was not replaced, neither was the Bishop of Wakefield, and these dioceses are now joined by that of Bradford to form a new diocese, that of Leeds. The new diocese has cathedrals in Ripon, Wakefield and Bradford. However, in addition to a Diocesan Bishop, there will be five Suffragan Bishops. Half a dozen bishops for one diocese. Maybe if there are cutbacks in dioceses like this rolling out steadily we shall finish up with Saint Theodore's originals plus a superabundance of bishops.

Over the last thirty years nationally, the percentage of those who claim to be Anglican has dropped from 40% to 20% of the population, in spite of the Church of England's efforts to be 'relevant' and 'meaningful' instead of 'holy'. I came across one way that the C of E is achieving such figures when I noticed this information from Ely Cathedral.

"Education visits at the Cathedral attracted nearly 10,000 students with a hugely popular Holiday Drop in every Monday and Wednesday during the school holidays offering a range of activities including arts, crafts, and storytelling.

The Pet Service takes place annually and is always well attended. The focus in recent years has been to present the Cathedral as a community resource, making the building a welcoming place for all. Last year more than 700 people attended the opening night of the Olympics which was shown on a big screen.

The Ely Cathedral Christmas Gift and Food Fair attracted 6000 people over two days, and the Flower Festival 20,000 over four days. There is also a week-long business exhibition in the Cathedral ('A Celebration of Business') attracting thousands of people and more than 150 local businesses as exhibitors. A spokeswoman from the Cathedral said "These are not just fund raising / money making events. They help bring people into the building, often for the first time, and once they have experienced the Cathedral they may return for a Service or wish to discover more. I think lay events such as these have helped increase overall attendance at our services and other liturgical events in the Cathedral.""

In the second half of the last century, Dean Patrick Hankey attracted people from all over the world to Ely through his personal wit and holiness. Today Saint Theodore would weep to see what his Church of England has come to. Juvenal says it all in Satire X, if you want the people to be on your side just give them 'bread and circuses'.

What I find bewildering is the absence of fundamental Christian principles within the modern Anglican church in the United Kingdom, ironically less so in other parts of the commonwealth. Party political influence, both from outside the church as well as within has neutralised its influence in both spheres. The goal of politicians of course is to ensure only they and they alone direct the ship of state.

Immanuel Kant proffered the view that the recognition of man as an end and not a means was the categorical imperative and that it could be discovered by reason alone. Kant claimed that the existence of reason itself is an intimation of God. If this be so, and accepted as it must be by the church of state in the UK then all men are equal to one another in their rights, which derive from God, and cannot be derived from other men. This concept of natural justice therefore, recognised in Magna Carta confirms the primacy of the individual, formed in the image of God. This view led to what Von Mises called modern economies, the industrial revolution in England and the huge advances for the living standards of the populace. It is the gradual removal of these rights in the last 50 years, not by law but regulation of which the church should surely be speaking out. Yet the Anglican Church's very silence makes them actually complicit in the move towards what Lord Mandelson described as the post democratic era.

Chapter 8

The Manipulation of Money

Perhaps the mightiest weapon of state oppression is money. There are all sorts of ways that politicians and their cronies manipulate money. This is because most people have no idea what money and banking is and how it works. Why should they? No school or university teaches it. Nor have they ever done so. Rothschild Communique June 25th 1863 New York, "The few who understand the system will be so interested in its profits, or so dependent upon its favours that there will be no opposition from that class. While on the other hand the great body of people, mentally incapable of comprehending the tremendous advantages will bear its burden without complaint and perhaps without suspecting that the system is inimical to their best interests".

Here is another, Henry Ford, "It is as well that the people of the nation do not understand our banking and monetary system, for if they did, I believe there would be a revolution before tomorrow morning."

Money, I reiterate is simply a medium of exchange, invented to replace barter, a cumbersome and impossible system of trade for a modern economy. Politicians do not comprehend this which is why they imagine if they print it in great quantity, all will be well. This is to completely misunderstand the role of money. I was

invited recently to give a lecture in a small English market town on my work on the 'Parliamentary' Economics and Monetary Affairs committee. I decided to challenge myself to make money, banking and inflation understandable to a willing, intelligent but lay audience. This is not as easy as it sounds. I have always found that I learn best when given an analogy to which I can relate. Better than graphs and formulaic computer models and all the rest of the paraphernalia that goes with the modern university economics course, so detached from reality even undergraduates are rebelling against it in England. As the great Von Mises explained, economics is about human action, for which no mathematical equation can account. I leave aside banking here as I want to concentrate on just money and how the state exploits it for themselves and their cronies.

Permit me to share the lecture with you here for I believe it covers the ground easily for victims of the system of whom there are many. A small market town is a magnificent microcosm of an economy. Indeed, in the days of the city-state one might argue it was the economic norm of the time.

Let us therefore take a walk down the high street to take in the scene, it is half a mile long. On one side there are shops - shops of every nature, bakers, cobblers, antiques, grocers, green grocers, a charity shop, pawn broker, chemist, toy shop and sports shop. Perhaps a dental surgery too. In this case it is a county town which means it is the regional political centre. On the other side are council offices, a veritable rabbit's warren of them. Each door has a plaque denoting which aspect of our lives they control (blight?) In the town I am in, the employees of the council considerably outnumber those in the shops. The 'high street' or 'retail' are suffering a sort of permanent depression. The supermarkets on the ring road have squeezed the life out of the town centre. The sheer economy of scale the big supermarkets can bring to bear is colossal. They provide 'free' parking, cheap fuel and a myriad of other attractions for the harassed shopper. Lined up against the high street are the forces of the state. First out is VAT at 20%. Then there is the business property tax, very significant in most English towns. Incidentally, the shopkeeper receives virtually nothing for this iniquitous burden. Parking is often made all but impossible. Where there is parking it is expensive and sinister uniformed town hall enforcers strut about waiting to pounce on the returning shopper late by even only a few minutes. The shopkeeper is also told by the state how much to pay their staff, what pension arrangements to make, what leave to give them and how many hours they may work. A small shopkeeper can be broken by a rogue employee under the draconian employment laws enacted always by those with no commercial experience.

There comes a limit to how much the government can borrow or tax. The market eventually intervenes. Investors eventually stop buying government bonds or tax simply grinds down the economy to a level where revenue plummets. The government, incidentally, enforce a legal tender policy, i.e. you can only use 'their' money, they then manipulate the system.

All major economies are now printing money. Corporate and social welfare is out of control in the industrial democracies and national debt is spiralling. The outstanding debt cannot possibly be repaid. In America, Japan, Australia, Eurozone and the UK the sums owed are beyond human understanding and rising by the day.

This is why there is now a major propaganda campaign to persuade people that inflation is a necessary and good requirement. This is of course absurd. Inflation is rising prices, deflation is falling prices. Go and stand in that High Street. Do you want the price of a loaf, eggs, butter, shoes, raincoats, bicycles, cars, hats etc to go up? Of course not. The state is preparing you for the inflation inevitably caused by printing money. At the moment the £350 billion electronically manufactured in the UK has not caused retail prices to inflate but asset prices. Property, stocks and bonds are inflated. Those asset rich get richer, at least on paper. This is the result of the chronological order of government-inspired inflation. You give the money to the banks who buy assets, mainly government bonds, easy money for the bankers so the bonuses continue to roll in. Especially as the bankers can only win. If they make bad calls the government transfer the loss to the taxpayer. As always, with government intervention, one section of society is favoured over another. What is extraordinary is that the section of society currently favoured are arguably the least deserving. Savers and pensioners are punished through low interest rates; borrowers, bankers, the already wealthy or the permanently unemployed win. The object of the exercise is to degrade the currency so that national debt is rendered meaningless because the currency is worthless.

Again walk down that high street. Who benefits? Public sector because their pensions are index-linked. They are ring-fenced in retirement. The bankers who receive the money first, before it becomes degraded. The hard-working middle England saver is crucified in later life with worthless savings and pensions. The wealth gap widens but not for the reasons most people understand. It is not laissez faire capitalism which creates the gulf but crony capitalism, politicians which benefit, bankers and the bureaucrats.

Observe the 'Too Big to Fail', propaganda campaign by the banks. Believe me I worked in the City or for City Institutions for forty years. The people there are too smart for politicians, civil servants and journalists. I was a fixed income professional investor and remember drinking with some old colleagues when the Irish Banks went under. They were all very glum because they were going to take some big hits on their portfolios. There was much talk of the value of their bonds falling to as little as 20p or 30p in the pound. They simply could not believe their luck when they woke up one morning and the 'haircut' had been transferred to the Irish taxpayer. This of course broke the Irish economy.

Young professional people cannot afford a house or flat in their country's national capital. This is a direct result of government interference with markets.

The plague of welfarism is reaching epidemic proportion. A very recent piece of research from a Washington think tank reveals there are now 148 million government beneficiaries in the US and 86 million full-time workers. The numbers are getting worse, debt is spiralling. The US has spent $3.7 trillion in the last 5 years. The new Medicaid programme is facing unfunded liabilities of more than £38 trillion for the generation born today. The number of Americans in food stamps now exceeds the entire population of Spain.

Europe spends an even higher proportion of GDP on welfare. Yet the silence is deafening and both the

Anglican and Catholic Church is calling for more. Does no one in public life have any sense of responsibility?

Wherever you look government is to blame for all the ills in the economy, here and abroad. The worse things become the more government invites you to rely on them to solve the problems of their own making. Young people in America are slowly beginning to realise this, fewer in Europe yet but growing.

Libertarianism is much more than 'smoking in the pub'. It is a whole new idea and way of life.

However, as Walter Bagelot so wisely told us, "One of the greatest pains to human nature is the pain of a new idea."

We must educate a whole new generation of journalists and television interviewers. They need to challenge the status quo. It is their job to protect us from the state as is the law of the land. At the time of writing one monster pharmaceutical company is proposing to buy another; there is speculation as to whether electronic cigarettes are good or harmful. If soft drinks contain too much sugar, the list is endless. We must learn to sweep away the fake debate on the subject at hand and ask the more important question, 'is this the role of government?' Are we children with the government acting in loco parentis. Is that the society we want? Why can't they leave us alone?

Ordinary people are severely damaged in the long term by artificially low interest rates. It is not only pensions and pensioners disadvantaged by false interest rates. Insurance companies depend on interest to cover claims, all types of insurance life, accident, employers, health with no yield they cannot operate in the long term. Big corporations and their cronies in banks and public service win by transfer of wealth to them from those who can least afford it.

Let us turn again to the high street. Sainsbury, Tesco, Aldi, Morrisons and their ilk have access to cheap capital unavailable to the small high street player. Big political party donations buy special favours. Economy of scale is equally effective in dealing with the myriad of staff employment problems. The big players perform an important role. They have brought quality and low prices to us all and good for them. The smaller companies can compete on a level playing field. Away then with VAT at 20% and the business rates, back to liberty of contract for employer and employees.

Give pubs a chance, remove duty from hand pulled beer, make it as cheap to drink in the pub as at home. There is much speculation as to why there is a continuing disparity in wealth distribution, much of it wrongheaded. It is the state and central banks who perpetrate the status quo, ring-fencing their favoured position at a cost to the rest of us. Guilt ridden politicians then increase the national minimum wage which simply means the high street shed yet more jobs or close altogether. The youngster, or indeed 'oldie' could exist on £6.50 per hour if his pint was not over £3, his cigarettes £7 and his diesel £1.40 per litre. Not to mention that dreaded 20% on everything else he buys.

If we do not grip these problems everything will be made in China and we will buy it online, although if we are not politicians, bureaucrats or bankers I do not know where the money will come from.

In short, the government printed £350 billion in the last 5 years. If you did not get any of it, you were or will be disadvantaged.

Appendix A

by Michael McManus

How we are Governed

In terms of how the UK is governed, it can be useful to see the stages a Bill passes through both Houses of Parliament before it becomes law. Draft Bills: A draft bill, as the name suggests is essentially a prototype law in simplified language. It allows the proposed law to be examined before presentation as a formal bill. This Draft Bill can be examined by committee at Westminster, either by select committees or joint committees. In popular language, Draft Bills are either referred to as Green Papers or White Papers. The former refers to laws that are more open to outside consultation and indicates possible future legislative action from the government, whilst the latter refers to a more concrete statement of legislative intent.

There are four types of Bill:

1) Public Bill: This refers to laws that have a national significance on the whole population, introduced by members Government ministers, who sit on the front benches at parliament.
2) Private Bill: This is a bill that would change the law, but only as it relates to specific individuals or companies. Parliament requires that any proposed Private Bill be prominently publicly advertised and

that individuals who will be affected by it be contacted. Please note a Private Bill is not to be confused with a Private Members Bill.
3) Private Members Bill: This refers to laws introduced by MPs who are not government ministers. Because these MPs sit on the rows of seats behind the Government Ministers, these MPs are often referred to as 'Back Benchers'. Because less time is allocated to debating and analysing these bills, they often do not end up being voted on and made into law.
4) Hybrid Bills: This refers to bills that, whilst significant for the whole population, are deemed to have particular significance for certain sections of the population. Examples of this would include the construction of the Channel Tunnel, and more recently, HS2. Hybrid Bills go through a longer Parliamentary debate procedure than other types of Bill, and impacted groups often address select committees as part of this process.

The passage of a Bill through the houses

Passage Through the Commons

First Reading: Firstly, a Bill is formally unveiled in the Commons, usually without debate.

Second Reading: The Bill is debated in the Commons, and if it passes a vote, can proceed to the next stage.

Committee Stage: This is whereby Committees relevant to the type of law being proposed debate amendments to the bill, with the committee chair choosing which ones are debated and voted on.

Report Stage: At this stage, the proposed law is debated again in the Commons, this time containing the amendments that have passed committee. These debates can last several days. The Speaker of the House selects amendments for discussion.

Third Reading stage: At this point, the bill can be debated, but no further amendments can be added, and debates must be focussed on what is actually in the bill, not what an MP would like to have seen. Once the debate is over, a vote is held to see if the Bill can proceed to the Lords.

Passage Through the Lords

At this stage, any Bill which has made it through the Lower House enters the Upper House. There is a broadly similar procedure here, though there are some differences:

First Reading: The Bill is formally announced in the Lords, without debate.

Second Reading: At this stage, Peers have their first chance to suggest changes and to speak in debates on the subject. Any Peer can participate.

Committee Stage: Peers then discuss the Bill in Committee. Amendments can be discussed, and there is no time limit on discussion.

Report Stage: There is more examination of the Bill at this stage, open to all Peers.

Third Reading: The Bill can then be voted on.

Final Stages

At this stage, the two Houses of Parliament can engage in what is known as 'Consideration of Amendments'.

Both Houses can recommend changes to the Bill. Only once both Houses agree can the Bill become law.

Royal Assent: This is the final stage in law-making. The Bill is signed by the reigning monarch, at which point it becomes known as an Act of Parliament, and becomes law.

European Law

The law-making process at European level is slightly different. The European Commission has the sole right to initiate legislation. The European Commission is divided into separate Directorate Generals (DG), each making law in a specific thematic area; DG Environment, DG Trade, DG Justice etc. There are a total of 33 DGs, staffed mostly by bureaucrats with legal training. The DGs operate with the assistance of so-called 'working groups', comprised mainly of technical experts and industry officials.

Following the passage of the Lisbon Treaty into law in 2009, the European Parliament has so-called ''co-decision powers' alongside the Council. This means both the Parliament and Council must be in agreement on a Commission proposal before it can become law.

The Council is where national Member States send Ministers to debate legislation. The meeting depends on exactly what is being discussed. For example, laws related to fishing will involve Fisheries Ministers meeting, laws related to Justice will involve Justice Ministers meeting etc.

One of the most important things to understand about the Council is that Member States have different voting weights, which is determined by their population;

* France, Germany, Italy, United Kingdom: 29 votes each
* Spain, Poland: 27 votes each
* Romania: 14 votes
* Netherlands: 13 votes
* Belgium, Czech Republic, Greece, Hungary, Portugal: 12 votes each
* Austria, Bulgaria, Sweden: 10 votes each
* Croatia, Denmark, Ireland, Lithuania, Slovakia, Finland: 7 votes each
* Cyprus, Estonia, Latvia, Luxembourg, Slovenia: 4 votes each
* Malta: 3 votes

There are several different ways decisions are voted on in the Council.

1) Simple Majority: This is whereby at least 15 member states are in favour. This often concerns votes related to procedural matters.
2) Qualified Majority Voting (QMV): Certain decisions require QMV decisions. In order to reach a QMV, two conditions must both be met. Firstly, at least 15 Member States must be in agreement, and secondly, this must amount to at least 260 votes. Theoretically, 15 Member States could object without their combined vote being at least 260.
3) Double Majority: This will be introduced in November 2014, and will apply for decisions for action related to the Foreign Common and Defence policies. This will require 55% of Member States and these 55% of Member States account for at least 65% of the EU population.

4) Unanimity: As the name suggests, all Member States must be in agreement on issues that require unanimity. One example of a policy that requires unanimity would be deciding whether or not to admit a new EU Member State.

The passage of the Lisbon Treaty had a significant impact on these decisions, such as changing the electoral mathematics required to achieve QMV thresholds, and changing the types of decision that required each type of voting procedure.

Appendix B

The Death of Democracy

In an interview promoting my book, *Guinea a Minute* on LBC Radio I referred to another book, the *Death of the God Democracy* by the German/American philosopher Hans Hoppe. To cut a long book short, he makes the point that the natural course of events with a democratic system is the danger of the electorate voting solely in their own interests. Leading inevitably to the demise of the system.

History is littered with examples, two of which are the demise of the Roman Empire and the collapse of the Weimar Republik. Debasement of the currency and national debt are the usual precursors to such a demise. The British very cleverly avoided the breakdown of their society be the enactment of the 1840 Reform Acts. For those who did not have the benefit of a traditional education, let me outline in a sentence or two how and why they came about.

Democracy in the 19th Century had stagnated; political power was largely in the hands of the aristocrats and landed gentry. The stories of 'rotten boroughs' makes fascinating reading today. For those interested, Antonia Fraser's brilliant book on Reform is well worth a fireside vigil.

The United Kingdom recognised that the main wealth of the nation was created by the new entrepreneurial middle class. They were grossly under-represented electorally, hence the Reform Acts to realign the balance and make the electorate more representative. This enlightenment has produced one of the most stable and long-term democracies in the world. Yet we find ourselves out of kilter 160 years on.

Our forebears could not have conceived of a nation state where 50% GDP was spent by government. A nation where there are more civil servants today than at the height of the British Empire, the largest the world has ever seen. The current electoral system is failing. In spite of a post war generation of peace and security, the British national debt is the highest in its history. The real figure carefully hidden by government is near 200% of GDP when public sector pensions and private funding initiatives are taken into account. Close to Greece, where society has almost broken down. Without German bailouts it would be destitute. We see the rise of fascism. Always the beneficiary of an economic collapse. The UK is bankrupt, there is no possible chance of debt repayment, we borrow £90 billion per year, we print billions of pounds which debases our currency.

How can the electoral system we have deliver salvation? 19 million homes in Britain are in receipt of some sort of welfare benefit. Out of 1.3 million people working for the NHS more than half have no medical qualification of any sort. Managers average £70,000 per year salary, nurses £30,000. Banks are nationalised to save their employees from the consequences of their own folly. We have benefit claimants who have never worked and have no intention of working, often neither did their parents. Thousands of local government workers earn more than £100,000 per year, landowners get millions of pounds in subsides, for just being landowners. Our mainstream politicians have no commercial experience, no idea how the wealth creating sector operates.

How can we arrest this economic and moral decline with an electoral system which gives a vote to anybody and everybody, who happens to be over eighteen years old? The system must reform; we need a complete reappraisal to reflect, as we did in the mid nineteenth century, more electoral power for those who create the revenue so disappointingly squandered by a bloated administration.

Is the system fair when a shop keeper pays rates on his house and his business, not to mention a heavy VAT and Income Tax bill and gets one vote. Some of his neighbours have contributed nothing to the national exchequer at all and maybe never will; they get one vote.

I do not expect to vote in a UNITE ballot because I am not a member and pay no dues. I do not expect a vote at Marks & Spencer's AGM because I am not a shareholder. We need to get to a system where the interest of the individual and the state are more compatible. Enlightened self-interest in the Adam Smith style. We need to do this now before society and the economy collapse. Let us at least start a national debate; they did all those years ago to our mutual benefit. We owe it to the next generation. The status quo is not an option.

All the BBC interviewers could manage was 'do you expect to be taken seriously?' What do you think dear reader? Over 150 years since we reviewed the UK franchise in depth. Clearly not worthy of debate on the BBC.

Appendix C

The Socratic Approach

The concept of compulsory quota was first mooted, if my memory serves me right, in the Women's Rights and Gender Equality Committee in 2005. The committee has a reputation of being eccentric by any standards, even by the bizarre standards of the EU. After nearly ten years as an EU 'Parliamentarian' I know that once an idea is suggested, no matter how implausible, it will eventually gain traction and approval, for the Brussels regulatory machine plays the long game. The compulsory female quota therefore will arrive sooner or later in some form. National states will roll over and give in to what they feel is inevitable, the people will shrug their shoulders and sigh believing that the great engine of law making will continue to spew forth belching smoke and poison like the old dark satanic mills of yesteryear.

Many words have been written on the subject of gender equality, feminism, quotas, research statistics, usually by social engineers. They claim resistance is archaic and futile. The intonation of voice, the flicker of the eyebrow, the sardonic conspiratorial glance to show solidarity with the 'sisterhood' by the female BBC TV presenter, herself a beneficiary of the quota system.

Yet my argument is not about the statistics which might show the experiment in Norway (40% quota now for female directors in public companies) has been a failure, which it appears to have been because as a retired investment strategist I know just how to manipulate statistics even if they were relevant to such an ephemeral debate.

My approach is Socratic. I believe most modern political thought and comment fails because society does not ask the right questions. This is possibly the fault of television, wireless and newspapers which are all part of the establishment. Penetrating questions on political philosophy or economics would expose the questioner as much as the questioned. How, for example, can public service broadcasting challenge government overspending when they are wasteful recipients of public largesse. How close can the Daily Telegraph or Sunday Times go to the wire to expose the failing of a Conservative administration? How could the Daily Mirror criticise the complete mismanagement of the economy or immigration in their term of office. German readers could no doubt fill in the names and parties of their cosy media government conspiracy of silence on the most important issues of the day.

I am always fascinated to hear pseudo philosophical scientific comment from the likes of Richard Dawkins, Brian Cox and the late Stephen Hawking on the impossibility of the creationist theory. Yet any senior physics professor will tell you that 95% of the universe remains unexplained, perhaps unexplainable? The atheist is an absurd figure, the agnostic is the only rational thinker. The answer is patently 'we don't know'. We may have a hypothesis or even a theory, but we do not 'know', how could we? What arrogance to suggest we do. Of course, 'faith' is a different concept and not the point at issue here. Or is it?

Let us assimilate such scanty evidence as we have to hand on the implications of enforced equality. Is that which is really on offer a system of engineering equality of outcome? Easier by far to achieve but of course there is no moral high ground here, even for a public service broadcaster who has long since had any form of original thought steamed out by the 'right-on politically correct' thought police.

Much of which we endure today on discussion of gender equality is the result of political fashion. This phenomenon is as familiar as haute cuisine or couture. Indeed, they bear direct comparison. Modern feminism was spawned in the bra burning 1970s by rather shrill, bored, middleclass women of a certain physical genre. They punched miles above their weight but represented few women.

Almost every woman of my mother's vintage in our avenue had military or naval service. Everything had been done by women that could possibly be done. Aircraft delivery pilots, truck driving, administration, front line nursing support. The Armistice Day service in our town was awash with ladies sporting war time medals. I have my mother's, still. My mother thought 'feminists' ridiculous, absurd and sometimes offensive.

So who do these women represent? Supported usually by men who seem to have no link with the usual social and sporting male preserves. The slightly effete politically correct chaps who get sand kicked in their face on the beach. You've guessed it. The middle class 'liberal' political elite. In most walks of life in America or Western Europe overt discrimination is actually illegal. Try advertising 'male applicant wanted must be under 30, strong, for heavy work, no blacks or Irish need apply'.

Yet the political class plough their own furrow. They have women only short lists. So discrimination is alright depending upon what type of discrimination it is; who are the actors? We therefore have a perpetuation of the system. Political women are in office because of the quota system. They are beneficiaries. They want more. If you lack merit why support a world which is meritocratic.

The core objection to 'affirmative action' in the field of gender 'equality' in commerce is that it is inherently immoral. Public companies are owned by shareholders who risk capital. The company must be run for their benefit and theirs alone. Of course, good business sense demands employees and customers are cared for but this is not the mission statement of any company, nor could it be. Everyone concerned and dependent on the well-being of a company must have the most meritocratic board members available. They may be tall, short, male, female, black, white, yellow, blond, brunette or red headed.

The idea that women need special political help to get to positions of authority is nonsense. Probably the most successful woman Chief Executive since the war was Kate Smith who turned around W H Smith, the ailing high street retailer in a sector which was thought to be in a terminal decline. Great Britain had a woman prime minister without a quota system, arguably the most successful peacetime prime minister of all time. I could continue with a list of successful women in a variety of fields but it is both patronizing and unnecessary.

Notwithstanding advance in neuro surgery, incidentally one of the leaders in this field is an Oxford lady surgeon, we know very little about the human mind. Least of all the difference between men and women.

Let us explore for a moment the questions needed to establish the difference between males and females. I am just about as 'Alpha' a male can be. Army, rugby, boxing, cricket, commerce etc. I am not 'new man', would not be caught dead at a birth of a baby and happy to punch the first man who tries to steal my beer. I had the opportunity to join the board of a FTSE 250 company in 1992. I worked in London, lived in Yorkshire travelled at weekends, worked a twelve hour day and was rarely at home. I was 42, had been married for about 5 years with no children.

I decided, after very careful thought, I did not want it. I enjoy hunting, fell walking, cycling, a bit of cricket and country pubs. Although very 'Alpha', not particularly ambitious and not motivated by money at all. I was on a package of about £70,000 per annum in 1992. No way big stuff by London standards but very liveable. Lifestyle quality is my goal. Most CEOs of FTSE 100 companies in my view are socially dysfunctional. They boast of never seeing their family and working 14 hour days and weekends. This is something to be ashamed of. Now I think that surely a very significant number of women would think the same. Especially with an inbuilt, genetic predisposition to give family higher priority. Perhaps the reason they are underrepresented in European boardrooms is because they are more balanced with different priorities. Who knows? We do know that if they choose to do it they are as competent as any male. What else do we know? That women are equally now represented in accountancy, law and medicine. Similarly, over-represented in certain professions. Radiography, physiotherapy, nursing, midwifery and social services. In short, lifestyle and career choices pretty well reflect where anyone with common sense would expect them to be. The small band of female political activists do not understand their own 'sisterhood'. Most professional and successful business women laugh at their views and antics although perhaps not as openly as I do. Political correctness is a funny sort of disease and political incorrectness a 'vice' which dare not speak its name.

There are many more unexplained differences between the sexes. Women, in spite of years of training in art and music, significant leisure time in the 18th and 19th Centuries have produced few great works. Although if I could have any picture on my drawing room wall it would certainly be by a woman. The estimable Lady Butler, worth googling unless you are French.

Men and women are different yet there is no golden rule. Most women can find the mustard in the pantry quicker than a man; most men can reverse a car better than a woman. Although my wife can reverse a horsebox through a narrow passage way better than most men. My female French colleague is a phenomenal car parker in tiny spaces in French cities. But it is not the norm.

Men and women care about different things on a micro-scale. Leaving the lavatory seat up, wet towels on the bed and the top left off the toothpaste will drive a wife made. A man simply cannot understand what the problem is. Most wives do not regard putting petrol in the car as any part of their responsibility. Men cannot see the point in making the bed if you are going to get back in it tonight.

Let me go further, as I must, to expose the absurdity of gender quotas for boardrooms, proposed by those with very little knowledge of life outside politics, never mind the commercial world. With 40 years of commerce, military and politics under my belt, I think I can offer a view based on experience. Italian army officers do not think like German officers. British officers do not think like most other European officers. American officers are quite unlike the British in spite of a common language and strong historical bond. But it grows more complicated still. The Northern Italian executive has a different nuanced view to the Southern, the Protestant Irish executive is poles apart from his Southern Irish Catholic opposite numbers. (In none of these examples do I suggest one is better than another). A London Human Resource Agency director is a completely different beast from the director of a ship building firm in Barrow in Furness.

A London professional woman has a completely different view and cultural approach to a Yorkshire professional. Notice I have not yet even attempted to illustrate the differences in social class. An upper middle class English woman has more in common with a French woman of her class than a working class British woman. A Japanese woman and a Singapore Chinese are about as different as it is humanly possible to be. So the whole concept of gender quota is no more sensible than having a quota system for size, complexion or hair colour. Indeed, what a paradox if there was discrimination based on race which is illegal in most industrialised democracies.

In France where the concept is advanced, rumour has it that it is working better than they thought it might. One is irresistibly drawn into speculation as to the role of the Chairman or Managing Director's mistress.

You cannot legislate for human nature, nor should you.

I received many letters from women, humorous and interesting, musing on the differences between the sexes. A subject of debate, theatre, anthropology and speculation since the dawn of time.

Janet Street-Porter, a sort of shrill journalist of the TV/tabloid genre screamed "Oaf". Not, I suspect, the best spokesperson for her sex. By the by, a word on 'offence', being offended an interesting phenomenon.

Yet a few months later James Gillespie of the Sunday Times was disparaging of John Gray's best seller "Men are from Mars, Women are from Venus". His criticism was it was a 'statement of the blindingly obvious'. Er – well yes, my point.

It would seem if I stood on the steps of my club and shouted "God Save the Queen" I would give offence. As I seem to be doomed to 'give offence' for eternity I thought it might be fruitful if I considered the modern usage of the term. The old chestnut for political abuse was 'fascist', that almost appears to be falling out of favour. The political and journalist class have long since abandoned any notion that fascism was a political creed, of enormous success in pre-war Italy and Spain, with significant support in other European countries. Simplistically it was a system that put the state first, citizen's last and formalised control over commerce. It was funded by state bond issue with no real prospect of sovereign debt repayment. Heavily centralised it was a Faustian pact between big business and senior politicians. Incidentally does it remind you of anything?

Offensive is the new derogatory term for the errant politician. Particularly useful for the anti-establishment classical liberal, libertarian so desperately feared by both the left and right in modern politics.

Let me outline the rules of the game. It is not possible within the game for anyone to be 'offended' if they are outside the cosy institutional cabal. Main stream politicians and journalists can write whatever they like, the outsider cannot claim to be offended. It is simply not a card he can play.

Both I and my family have been regularly vilified in so many different ways I have lost count.

Epilogue

Many years ago I learned at the Ashridge Business College that in management and corporate training when one finished a course of lectures delegates should be left with 'the doing thing'. It is one thing to analyse problems, discuss and debate them but at least some solutions have to be offered. Let us therefore articulate the obstacles society has, not just in the UK but in the industrialised, democratic world.

The great barrier to solutions is the failure of the state in almost every area of endeavour. This is almost always a result of interference with the market. Who or what is the market? Well of course it is people. People left free to make their own judgements, indeed make their own mistakes. Interference always creates more problems than it solves. The market is a self-correcting phenomenon. Whenever I see or hear the expression market forces it is usually nothing of the kind. The banking collapse was due simply to a flawed system, fractional reserve. A central bank compounding the failure, and criminal political support for it utilising taxpayers' money. The US, UK and Ireland rescued bankers who should have been sent to prison, with maintenance of the status quo the bonus party goes on. 150 years ago in America those bankers would have been hanged and rightly so. Politicians who are equally culpable still strut the world stage, either seeking re-election or posing as elder statesmen. Some charging thousands of dollars for a lecture. One wonders who would attend a lecture for money by failed politicians and bureaucrats.

In education we have the same problem. Box ticking, state education has been a disaster. Thousands of parents beggar themselves to remove their children from it. The industrial democracies seem incapable of running education. Instead of being for the benefit of children and parents it is for the idle advantage of Teachers' Unions. Equally true of the US, not just the UK. Teaching should be a privilege and vocation. Look at the NUT representatives at their conference. Would you put your beloved offspring into their charge? Ear ringed, bearded, scruffy, foam flecked and interested in only their salary and pensions at the taxpayers' expense. When did they last talk of children or parents? It must be swept away and the market, i.e. parents, must be given their choice. Return immediately the taxpayer's contribution to state education to parents and allow them to make the choice. Those who believe the state should educate children can send them to such schools that still remain. We must retreat from the absurd situation where every youngster needs a Mickey Mouse degree from a state university to be called for interview to any white-collar job. What is the point of a 2:1 in philosophy, economics or politics? All the state produces are youngsters of twenty two or three with no idea what they want to do or why. Youth unemployment means post graduate courses and further degrees in nothing of importance and now the youth is no longer a youth but an adult, twenty five years old and totally unfitted for the world. Vocational and professional training should start at seventeen if the western democracies are going to compete with the Pacific Rim economies. University is for real academics. Let us develop our classicists, historians and mathematicians, but significantly fewer in number. This will improve standards and therefore morale amongst those who remain in the system. I would argue the UK could support twenty real universities and I would remove state funding from them. Let there be a tax system which supports philanthropy and see our universities funded by endowments. Big business would be happy to sponsor the research training hospitals and universities with profit released from the tax burden. The whole system would be genuinely market driven.

It was argued that the emphasis in late Victorian education on script for the lower middle classes was to build a nation of clerks to administrate empire and commerce. I would argue the current education system is to prepare the electorate for the post-democratic era. How else could I lecture to university history and economics undergraduates who had never heard of Herbert Spencer, Frederic Bastiat or Murray Rothard?

It also would seem undergraduates are not trained how to think. There is almost no interest in challenging the status quo. The state will provide. This is natural enough, a sixth former or undergraduate has never had to contribute to his own well-being. The modern gilded youth is paid for by parents and the state, food, rent, education appear as if by magic. They have never received a tax bill or been confounded by the petty bureaucracy their parents face. Children of small businessmen are often the exception to this rule and more aware of the daily struggle their parents endure. Many believe that the status quo was ever thus, not understanding the government's interference in our daily lives and the incumbent monster spending and borrowing is a relatively new phenomenon. Nor do they have any notion of how expensive 'free' is to the community. Education, health and welfare are cripplingly expensive and the burden is born by the ever-diminishing number of wealth creators in society. Who is the wealth creator? Anyone who does not work directly or indirectly for the state. The humble one girl hair dresser is a wealth creator, the bloated bureaucracy in the Town Hall drains her of her hard-earned money, much of which is siphoned off to plague her with regulations.

The national health system is desperate for reform. It has 2.2 million employees, less than half of whom have any medical qualifications. Over £140 billion pounds per annum in costs. Nothing free about it. Yet it is the sacred cow of British politics. It will remain so unless the next generation is taught how to think, how to challenge.

It is not just a generation of Brits who do not have these skills, a system of state broadcasting compounds the problem. Many of the major burdens on the long-suffering public are completely ignored by a state system which, under its own charter, is obliged to inform and entertain. There has never been on the BBC a serious challenge to membership of the EU, progressive taxation, the concept of the NHS or state education (not programmes about failing schools, but the concept that education should be the role of government). Where are the programmes explaining the extent of government debt, the dangers of money printing and the hidden costs of future social welfare to the next generation?

Is, as Hans Hoppe believes, democracy doomed to failure? Certainly with a welfare state and an electorate whose eligibility criterion is being eighteen years old, failure is inevitable.

The question we must all ask ourselves is do we believe the state can make better and more informed decisions for our families than we can? Can government spend our money more wisely than us? What is the legitimate remit of government and its politicians? Has the current system, arguably in its current form since 1945, been successful? If so, exactly how?

What if anything are people prepared to give up in exchange for an improved material lifestyle? Small states seem to perform better than large even if authoritarian. Increased personal wealth, along with lower crime and a cleaner environment such as Switzerland or Singapore present an attractive option. Many Pacific Rim countries run perfectly sound and successful education systems. Yet is this enough for the human spirit? Do we value freedom of action and speech over material wealth, are they incompatible? History would suggest the greatest advancement in science, medicine, incomes and standard of living for everyone has come about when government was small, taxes were low and the individual under law prospered.

Perhaps the 'doing thing' for all of us now is to challenge the status quo, from the ground up.

People feel government interferes with their lives too much. Every aspect of their daily lives seems to be affected by politicians or their enforcement agencies. Amazing, is it not, that people felt this way in 1850? What would Victorians have made of modern Britain or indeed modern America? The Englishman, so protective of his freedoms both personal and religious, won at such expenses in blood. The Americans and that famous frontier spirit originally founded by those who sailed through such adversity to found a new nation.

Societies built on the entrepreneurial and adventurous spirit have fallen prey to bureaucrats. Can the people who run California really be the heirs of the 'Forty Niners'? Those who won the west. In Australia, also stifled by bureaucracy and regulation only one hundred and fifty years ago today the forebears of health and safety inspectors were circumventing the globe to set up homesteads in the outback. It seems countries are built by risk, hard work and sacrifice when all the hardships are over the Jobsworth politicos and administrators glide in like so many vultures to feed off a carcass still breathing.

Let me float an idea first conceived a hundred and fifty years ago.

Imagine if you will a Libertarian ID card, a cross between a passport and a credit card. A Laissez Passer if you prefer. This card would abrogate the state of its self-imposed responsibilities to the citizen. It would be carried at all times. It would be recognised by a computerised system held at every cash or point of sale point. The application for such a pass would involve signing a consent form, simplistically 'I want nothing from the state in any way, I do not therefore expect an invoice from the state in any form'.

Let your imagination run riot. You tear up your rates bill, you will dispose of your own waste, your children go to private school, you have a soak away system but if it is not appropriate you will pay a company to provide the needful. You can use the highway because you have paid for your road tax disc. You go shopping, you buy a caravan for the annual family holiday, your card absolves you from VAT at 20% (£3,000 off the average van), the caravan company are delighted incidentally because VAT is killing their factory. You get your payslip, no NI or PAYE.

In my case a return cheque from HMRC of £13,651 income tax and £2,000 NI. My employer of course also gets a further £5,000 in reduced employer NI.

Pensions and health?

I have just got £20,000 extra every year and my high street purchases, big or small, have all been sold to me at a 20% discount. I can also afford to join the district security system, away with the police whom I never see anyway.

I fill up my car, a Peugeot 308. Normally £75. Bingo it is now only £20! I celebrate with a pint, no longer £3 but £1.20 which is what the gaffer can now sell it to me for. I could continue, but you get the point.

Who, I wonder, would not register? What about the genuinely infirm, those who simply cannot provide for themselves? Middle England has now been relieved of the crippling burden under which it has laboured for so long. Philanthropy booms as it once did, mutual societies, benefit societies, public parks, free hospitals in the real sense of the word. Everything we enjoy of any value today and not created by government but private enterprise. Your microwave, refrigerator, motor car, computer, mobile phone, TV. The state created none of this. I quote again from Murray Rothbard, "The state is an institution of theft writ large".

Bibliography

A History of Western Philosophy – Bertrand Russell
We Hold These Truths – Mortimer J Adler
For a New Liberty. The Libertarian Manifesto – Murray N Rothbard
The Art of Suppression. Pleasure, Pain and Prohibition since 1800 – Christopher Snowden
Edwardian Requiem. A Life of Sir Edward Grey – Michael Waterhouse
Perilous Question. The drama of the Great Reform Bill 1832 – Antonia Fraser
Great British Weather Disasters – Philip Eden
Great Minds of the Western Intellectual Tradition – Great Courses. The Teaching Company
Liberty Through Gold. A slave revolt in the world empire of paper money kings – Professor Dr. Hans J Bocker
John Maynard Keynes: Fighting for Britain 1937 – 1946 – Robert Skidelsky
The Money Bubble. What to do before it pops – James Turk & John Rubino
Social Statics or the Conditions Essential to Human Happiness Specified and the first of them Dev – Herbert Spencer
The Day Lincoln Was Almost Shot – Benjamin Franklin Cooling
The Origins of the Common Law – Arthur R Hogue
Burning our Money – Mike Denham

Human Action – Ludwig von Mises
The Real Lincoln – Thomas J Dilrenzo
Road Accidents. Prevent or Punish? – JJ Leeming
Inflation Tax: The Plan to deal with the debts – Pete Comley
Democracy. The God That Failed – Hans-Hermann Hoppe
Chill: A reassessment of global warming theory – Peter Taylor
The Anglosphere Challenge – James C Bennett
Heaven & Earth. Global Warming the Missing Science – Ian Plimer
The Great Rebellion – Ivan Roots
The Rise of Political Lying – Peter Oborne
Lord Denning A Biography (2nd Edition) – Edmund Heward
Full Disclosure – Andrew Neil
The Welfare State We're In – James Bartholomew
Constitutional Money – Richard H Timberlake
The Rational Optimist – Matt Ridley
The Austrian School – Jesús Huerta de Soto
The Bastiat Collection (2nd Edition) – Claude Frederic Bastiat
Cool It – Bjorn Lomborg
Climate: The Counter Consensus – Professor Robert M Carter
When will the lights go out? – Derek Birkett
Nullification: How to resist Federal tyranny in the 21st Century – Thomas E Woods, Jr
The Case for Legalizing Capitalism – Kel Kelly
Once there was an Empire - Alan Bloom
Mises on Money - Gary North
The History of the Decline and Fall of the Roman Empire – Edward Gibbon

Godfrey Bloom's Biography

Godfrey Bloom began his career in the City of London in 1967. His subsequent 35 years were extremely varied, probably impossible now in a very much more specialized and regulated city financial service environment. He won international awards for fund management.

Godfrey retired from investment management in 2004 to take up his seat in the European 'Parliament'. He sat as an independent representing Yorkshire and North Lincolnshire. In 2006 he gave a very prescient paper to the National Defence University of Washington on procurement forewarning of the crisis to come.

Mr Bloom has a very long record of accurate prediction. In the mid nineteen nineties as a guest lecturer at Cambridge University he predicted the failure of the Euro over a ten year period. He is a long -term critic of prescriptive regulation. He led the British opposition vote to Brussels governed regulation in the European Parliament in September 2010. Recent speaking engagements have included the advent of Basel III banking regulation in London, Vienna and Warsaw. He is a popular speaker at universities and enjoyed amongst others, engagements at Durham, Newcastle, St. Andrews, Oxford, London, Syracuse and York universities, the Mises Institute in Alabama,

Fórum da Liberdade in Brazil and Joint Services Staff College in Shrivenham.

His uncompromising views on the current financial crisis enjoy popularity on foreign television networks, but, of course, not the BBC who regard his anti Keynesian views as too hot to handle.

He served 30 years with the Territorial Army, initially with the County of London Yeomanry and holds the Territorial Decoration and bar, Sovereign's and at bar. He is also a senior graduate of the Armed Forces Parliamentary Scheme & Associate Member of the Royal College of Defence Studies.

Mr Bloom has more views on his speeches than any other MEP in the history of the Parliament in one year. The first elected politician to question the apocryphal man-made global warming hypothesis on British TV in 2006. He also produced a film on the absurdity of wind turbines as an energy solution for Western Europe.

He is married to one of England's leading equine physiotherapists.

www.godfreybloom.uk
www.europesillwind.org
Facebook: @godfreybloomofficial
Twitter: @goddersbloom

CPSIA information can be obtained
at www.ICGtesting.com
Printed in the USA
BVHW031544130819
555787BV00001B/49/P